Atlas of the Bible Lands

Edited by
Harry Thomas Frank
Late Professor of Religion, Oberlin College

Consultant for Revised Edition
Roger S. Boraas
Professor of Religion, Upsala College

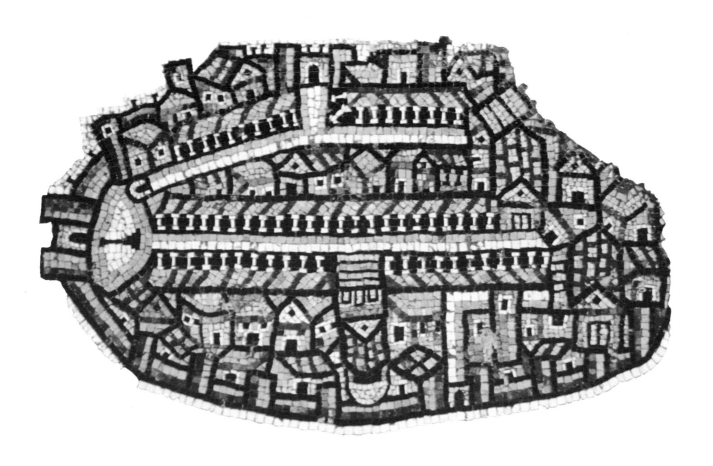

HAMMOND INCORPORATED   MAPLEWOOD, NEW JERSEY

Title Page illustration:
Detail of Jerusalem from the Medeba
mosaic map. The Damascus Gate is at
the far left. The mosaic dates from about
A.D. 560 and is the oldest map of the
Holy Land.

Wall painting from tomb at Beni-hasan
depicts Asian people, probably Amorites,
entering Egypt about 1900 B.C.

ATLAS OF THE BIBLE LANDS, Revised Edition
Entire contents © Copyright 1990, 1984, 1977
by HAMMOND INCORPORATED
All rights reserved. No part of this book may
be reproduced or utilized in any form or by any
means, electronic or mechanical including photo-
copying, recording or by any information storage
and retrieval system, without permission in writing
from the publisher.

The maps "Routes in Palestine" and "Economy of
Palestine" on pages 5 and 7 were prepared especially for
Abingdon Press and published in The Interpreter's
Dictionary of the Bible, Supplementary Volume. *They are*
reproduced here with Abingdon's permission.

Library of Congress Cataloging-in-Publication Data

Hammond Incorporated.
    Atlas of the Bible Lands.

    Includes index.
      1. Bible—Geography—Maps.   I. Frank, Harry Thomas.
II. Boraas, Roger S.   III. Title.
G2230.H3   1990   220.9'1   89-675129
ISBN 0-8437-7056-2 case bound edition
ISBN 0-8437-7055-4 soft cover edition
Printed in the United States of America

Contents

Preface to the Revised Edition

THE BIBLE speaks to every human being. For believers —Jewish, Christian or Muslim—it sets the basic perceptions of God, human life, history, and meaning. Its ideas and images have permeated art, music and philosophy to become fundamental to any modern view of human wisdom, whether in support of or challenge to current ideas. So it belongs to and affects all humans.

The Bible is also a very specific, down-to-earth book. Like all of us it is rooted in time and place. This is part of its strength. It reaches people where they are—in this world, of this time. Unlike many speculative religions, which project worlds and meanings from emotions or spectacular imaginations, the Bible deals with folks who are born, learn, work, fight, marry, rejoice, weep, struggle and die. It declares the meaning of our shared life, our common experience, our present dangers, our hopes, our sense of purpose. In that it is God's Word to people.

So, through the Bible we follow Moses to Mt. Sinai (Exodus 19). We hear Deborah's victory song at Taanach (Judges 5). We see David dance on the way to Jerusalem (2 Samuel 6). We find Jeremiah wondering if God has abandoned him (Jeremiah 15). We hear the anguish of defeated Judeans in exile in Babylon (Psalm 137). We accompany Nehemiah on his evening inspection of the ramparts and gates of Jersualem (Nehemiah 2:11). We rejoice with Simeon at the birth of a new baby boy (Luke 2:22-32). We hear Jesus' stories about the Kingdom of God (Luke 15). We walk with a man down 4,000 feet in 18 miles from Jerusalem to Jericho and see him mugged on the road (Luke 10:30). We struggle with Paul on the way from Jerusalem to Damascus (Acts 9) and endure with him the storm and ship damage off Crete (Acts 27). In such matters the Bible speaks to us of events and meaning in specific places and times no matter where or when we live.

However, the times are remote (two or three thousand years ago), and the places are unfamiliar, frequently having strange names (Ur, Mizpah, the Kishon or Jabbok rivers). Having a realistic sense of those Biblical places helps sharpen our awareness of what the Bible says. Why would Abraham leave Ur or Haran and move to Shechem? Why did Israelites avoid the easy coast road in leaving Egypt at the Exodus? Why did David pick Jerusalem for the capital of his new kingdom? Geography, history and the sense of God's will are entwined closely in the Bible. Revelation of God's promises and warnings came to people through experiences in particular places at particular moments. Later reflections recall that meaning, sometimes embraced in recollections of the places and specific mention of the times.

With the help of this newly revised *Hammond's Atlas of the Bible Lands* the places may be found on easily readable up-to-date maps. The settings of the stories are richly illustrated. Maps, plans and photos combine to bring to the reader an immediate perception of the places in which the significant events occurred. The organization by time periods is aided by charts showing what happened in different parts of the Biblical world at the same time. They set the Biblical story against the backdrop of contemporary political developments. All this helps us follow the Biblical story from the earliest ancestors of Israel through the founding of the churches of the second century A.D. It reminds us that the places of knowing God are the places of earth, of our ordinary life.

R.S.B.

Upsala College, June 1989

. . . the land which you are going over to possess is a land of hills and valleys, which drinks water by the rain from heaven, a land which the Lord your God cares for; the eyes of the Lord your God are always upon it, from the beginning of the year to the end of the year.
—Deuteronomy 11:11-12

How to use this Atlas

Arrangement

This Atlas begins with an introductory section on the unique geography of the Holy Land. Besides terrain, vegetation and climate information, there are maps on trade routes and the economy of Palestine. The main collection of maps is arranged chronologically using the Biblical record from the Old and New Testament with a focus primarily on Palestine. The viewpoint broadens at appropriate intervals, to include the larger areas of the Ancient Near East and Greek and Roman worlds. These maps show important political changes, the course of empires and the expansion of the early Christian Church.

Also of special interest in the main collection of maps are the detailed plans of the Holy City of Jerusalem at critical points in Biblical history as well as reconstructions of other cities, ancient sites, battles and even buildings.

The last section of the Atlas brings the reader into the present with an essential look at the lands of the bible in modern times, along with an up-to-date map of major archaeological sites in Israel and Jordan. The time charts and the gazetteer-index at the back of the book are valuable reference tools for locating events in both time and place.

Place-names

The spellings of Biblical sites and geographical names used in the maps and index are those found in the Revised Standard Version (RSV) of the Bible. Alternative Biblical or other ancient names are placed in parentheses. A question mark following a site name indicates the location is possible or probable but not yet certain.

Names of political regions, empires, kingdoms and provinces are shown in large boldface capitals, e.g. **BABYLONIA**.

Names of tribal and ethnic groups are usually in lighter typeface, e.g. ARAMEANS.

Cities and towns are in lower case roman type, e.g. Tyre.

Seas, lakes, rivers, etc. are in lower case italic, e.g. *The Great Sea* , with later or modern place names in parentheses, e.g. *(Mediterranean Sea)*.

Mountain ranges are shown in italic capitals, e.g. *CAUCASUS*; mountain peaks are in lower case italics, e.g. *Mt. Tabor* .

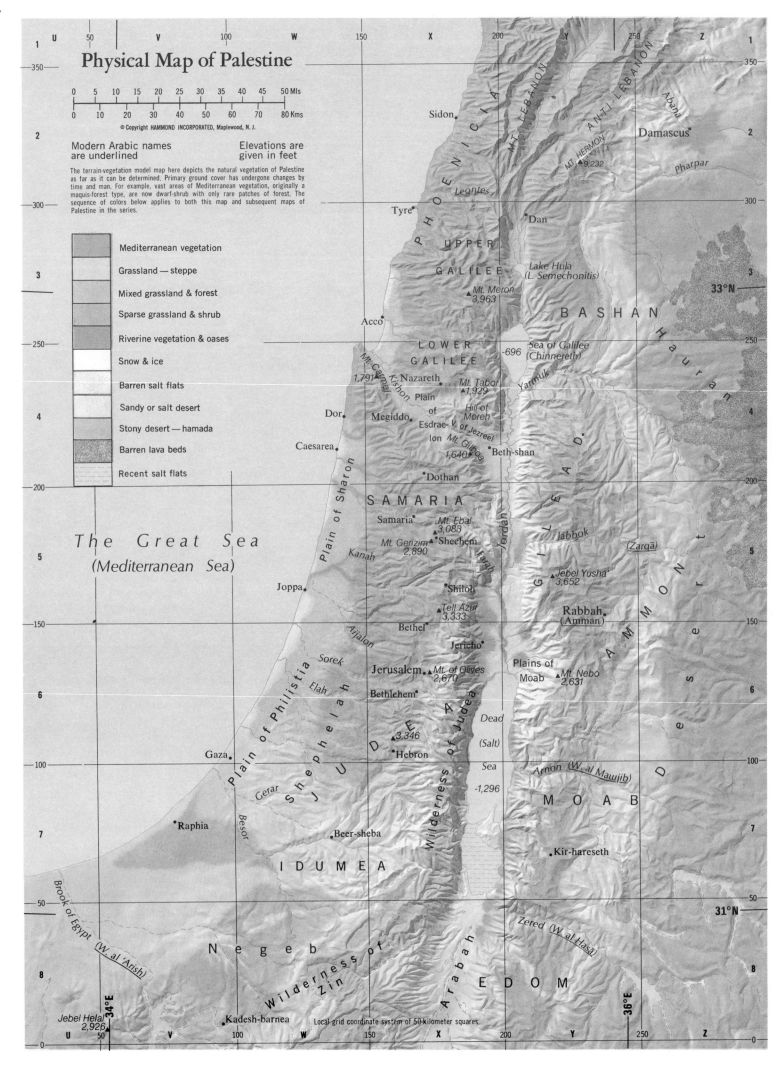

Physical Map of Palestine

| 0 | 5 | 10 | 15 | 20 | 25 | 30 | 35 | 40 | 45 | 50 MIs |
| 0 | 10 | 20 | 30 | 40 | 50 | 60 | 70 | 80 Kms |

© Copyright HAMMOND INCORPORATED, Maplewood, N.J.

Modern Arabic names are underlined   **Elevations are given in feet**

The terrain-vegetation model map here depicts the natural vegetation of Palestine as far as it can be determined. Primary ground cover has undergone changes by time and man. For example, vast areas of Mediterranean vegetation, originally a maquis-forest type, are now dwarf-shrub with only rare patches of forest. The sequence of colors below applies to both this map and subsequent maps of Palestine in the series.

- Mediterranean vegetation
- Grassland — steppe
- Mixed grassland & forest
- Sparse grassland & shrub
- Riverine vegetation & oases
- Snow & ice
- Barren salt flats
- Sandy or salt desert
- Stony desert — hamada
- Barren lava beds
- Recent salt flats

The Great Sea
(Mediterranean Sea)

Local grid coordinate system of 50-kilometer squares.

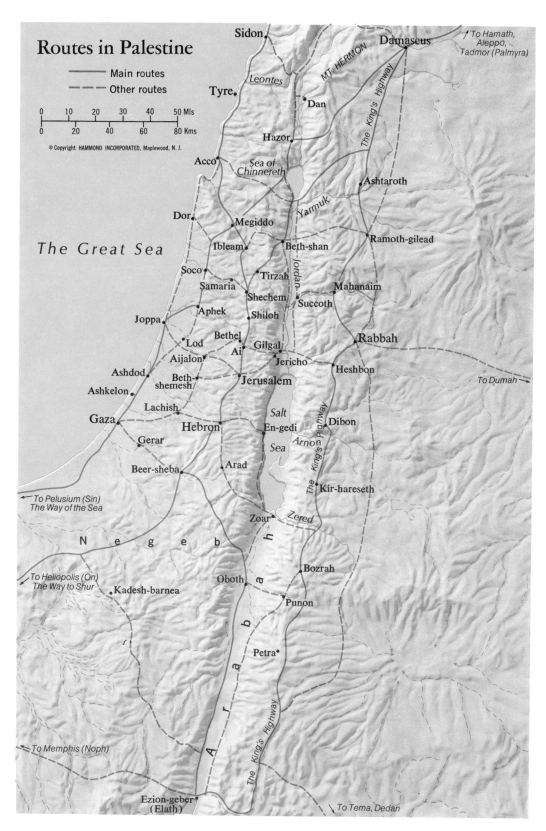

Routes in Palestine

Main routes
Other routes

0 10 20 30 40 50 Mls
0 20 40 60 80 Kms

© Copyright HAMMOND INCORPORATED, Maplewood, N.J.

Sidon
Damascus
To Hamath, Aleppo, Tadmor (Palmyra)
MT. HERMON
Leontes
Tyre
Dan
The King's Highway
Hazor
Acco
Sea of Chinnereth
Ashtaroth
Dor
Yarmuk
Megiddo
Ibleam
Beth-shan
Ramoth-gilead
Soco
Tirzah
Jordan
Samaria
Mahanaim
Shechem
Succoth
Aphek
Shiloh
Joppa
Bethel
Rabbah
Lod
Gilgal
Ai
Aijalon
Jericho
Ashdod
Beth-shemesh
Jerusalem
Heshbon
To Dumah
Ashkelon
Lachish
Salt
Gaza
Hebron
En-gedi
Dibon
The King's Highway
Gerar
Sea
Arnon
Beer-sheba
Arad
Kir-hareseth
To Pelusium (Sin) The Way of the Sea
Zoar
Zered
N e g e b
To Heliopolis (On) The Way to Shur
Oboth
Bozrah
Kadesh-barnea
Punon
Petra
The Great Sea
The King's Highway
To Memphis (Noph)
A r a b a h
Ezion-geber (Elath)
To Tema, Dedan

The Plain of Esdraelon looking north toward Mount Tabor.

Goats graze in the forbidding central Samaria hills, where the invading Hebrews found a home for their flocks in Biblical times.

Today children frolic in the cool waters beneath the waterfalls of En-gedi, celebrated in the Song of Songs.

The placid Dead Sea looking eastward toward the hills of Transjordan. Wind erosion at this lowest spot on earth produces an eerie, lunar landscape along the western shore.

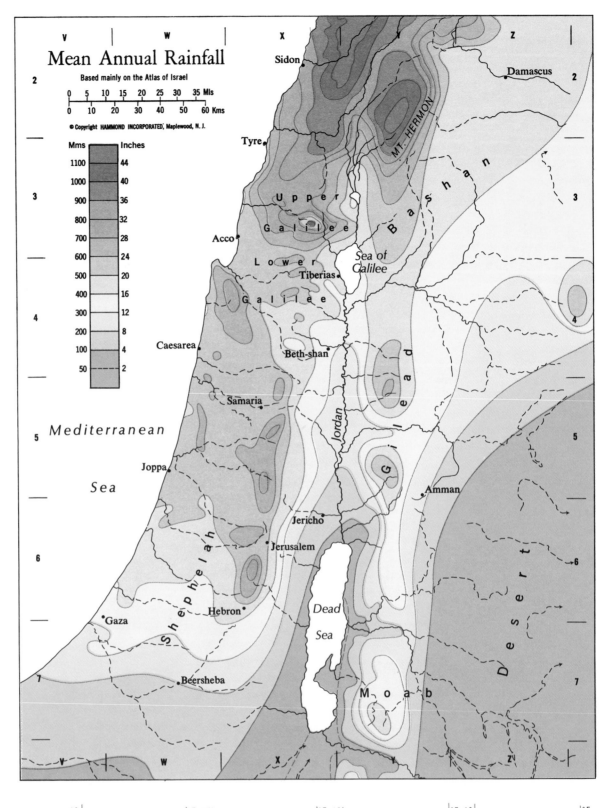

Mean Annual Rainfall

Based mainly on the Atlas of Israel

Temperature, rainfall,
and relative humidity
for selected stations

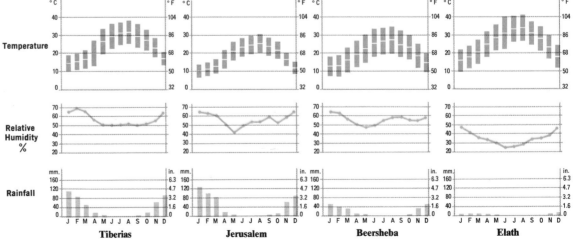

Sources: World Climatic Data, 1972; Statistical Abstract of Israel, 1969

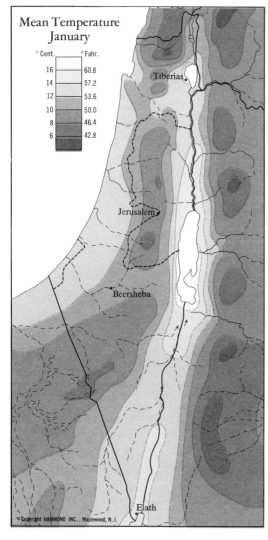

Mean Temperature January

° Cent.	° Fahr.
16	60.8
14	57.2
12	53.6
10	50.0
8	46.4
6	42.8

Tiberias
Jerusalem
Beersheba
Elath

© Copyright HAMMOND INC., Maplewood, N.J.

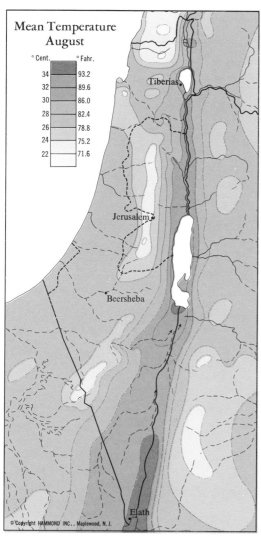

Mean Temperature August

° Cent.	° Fahr.
34	93.2
32	89.6
30	86.0
28	82.4
26	78.8
24	75.2
22	71.6

Tiberias
Jerusalem
Beersheba
Elath

© Copyright HAMMOND INC., Maplewood, N.J.

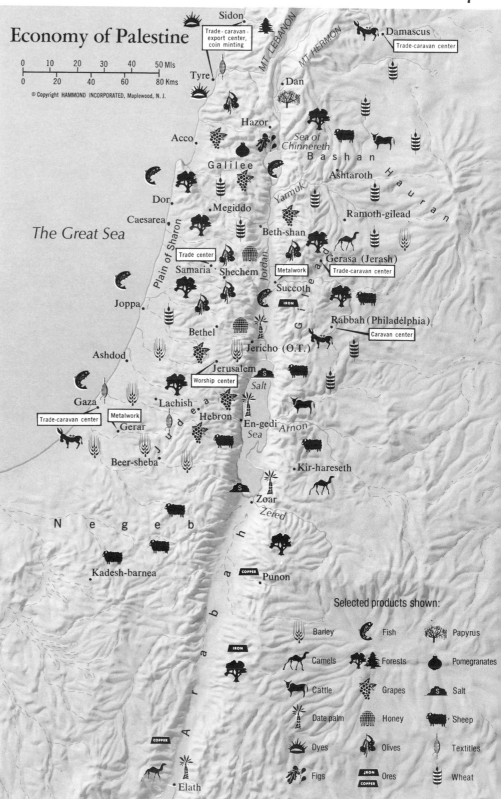

Economy of Palestine

0 10 20 30 40 50 Mls
0 20 40 60 80 Kms

© Copyright HAMMOND INCORPORATED, Maplewood, N.J.

Selected products shown:

Barley, Fish, Papyrus, Camels, Forests, Pomegranates, Cattle, Grapes, Salt, Date palm, Honey, Sheep, Dyes, Olives, Textitles, Figs, Ores, Wheat

Grapes being weighed in a manner reminiscent of a period when both kings and prophets in Israel were concerned with honest measure.

A cluster of dates suggests the richness and plenty of well-watered date palm plantations such as those at Jericho.

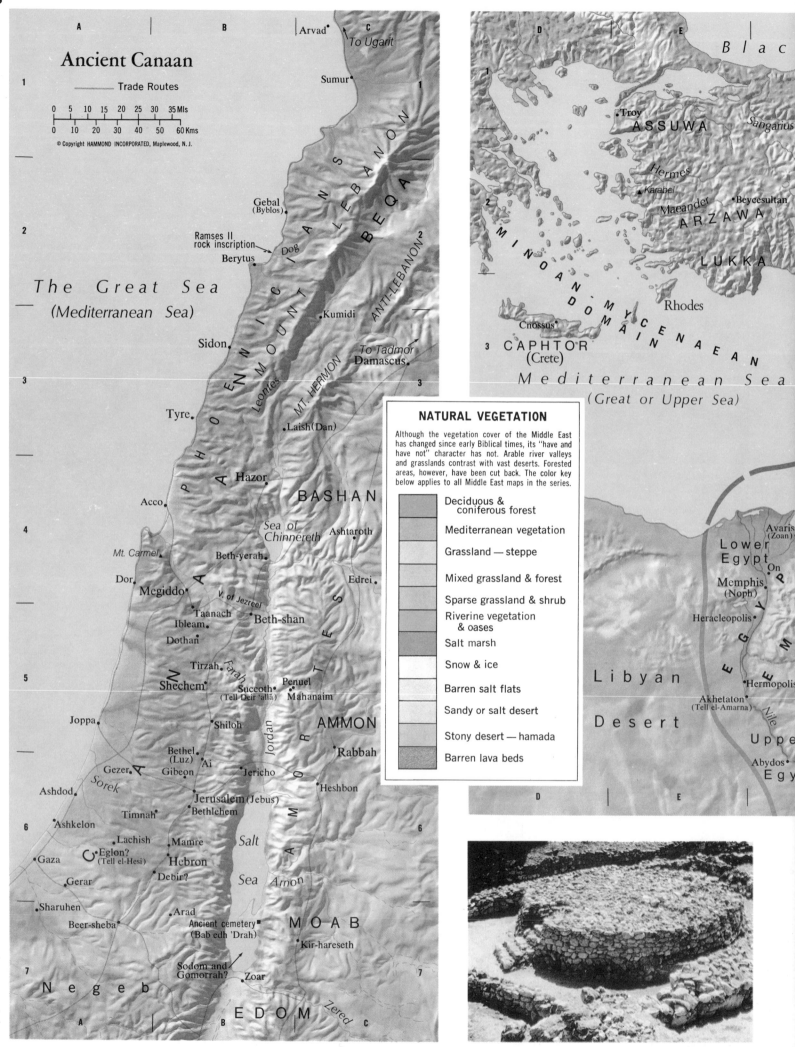

Ancient Canaan

—— Trade Routes

0 5 10 15 20 25 30 35 Mls
0 10 20 30 40 50 60 Kms
© Copyright HAMMOND INCORPORATED, Maplewood, N. J.

The Great Sea
(Mediterranean Sea)

Arvad
To Ugarit
Sumur

L E B A N O N   M O U N T A I N S
B E Q A
A N T I - L E B A N O N

Gebal
(Byblos)
Ramses II
rock inscription
Dog
Berytus

Kumidi

To Tadmor
Damascus

Sidon
MT. HERMON
Leontes

Tyre
Laish(Dan)

Hazor
BASHAN
Acco
Sea of
Chinnereth
Ashtaroth
Mt. Carmel
Beth-yerah
Dor
Edrei
Megiddo
V. of Jezreel
Taanach
Beth-shan
Ibleam
Dothan
Tirzah
Farah
Shechem
Succoth
Penuel
(Tell Deir 'allā)
Mahanaim
Joppa
AMMON
Shiloh
Jordan
Bethel
(Luz)
Ai
Rabbah
Gezer
Gibeon
Sorek
Jericho
Heshbon
Ashdod
Jerusalem(Jebus)
Timnah
Bethlehem
Ashkelon
Salt
Lachish
Mamre
Eglon?
Gaza
(Tell el-Hesi)
Hebron
Sea
Gerar
Debir?
Arnon
Sharuhen
Arad
Beer-sheba
Ancient cemetery
MOAB
(Bab edh 'Drah)
Kir-hareseth
Sodom and
Gomorrah?
Zoar
N e g e b
E D O M
Zered

P H O E N I C I A
A M M O R I T E S

B l a c
D   E
Troy
ASSUWA
Sangarius
Hermes
Karabel
Beycesultan
Maeander
ARZAWA
LUKKA
Rhodes
MINOAN
Cnossus
AND
CAPHTOR
MYCENAEAN
(Crete)
DOMAIN
M e d i t e r r a n e a n   S e a
(Great or Upper Sea)

Avaris
(Zoan)
Lower
Egypt
On
Memphis
(Noph)
Heracleopolis
Libyan
Hermopolis
Akhetaton
(Tell el-Amarna)
Desert
Upper
Abydos
Egy
E G Y P T

NATURAL VEGETATION

Although the vegetation cover of the Middle East has changed since early Biblical times, its "have and have not" character has not. Arable river valleys and grasslands contrast with vast deserts. Forested areas, however, have been cut back. The color key below applies to all Middle East maps in the series.

- Deciduous & coniferous forest
- Mediterranean vegetation
- Grassland — steppe
- Mixed grassland & forest
- Sparse grassland & shrub
- Riverine vegetation & oases
- Salt marsh
- Snow & ice
- Barren salt flats
- Sandy or salt desert
- Stony desert — hamada
- Barren lava beds

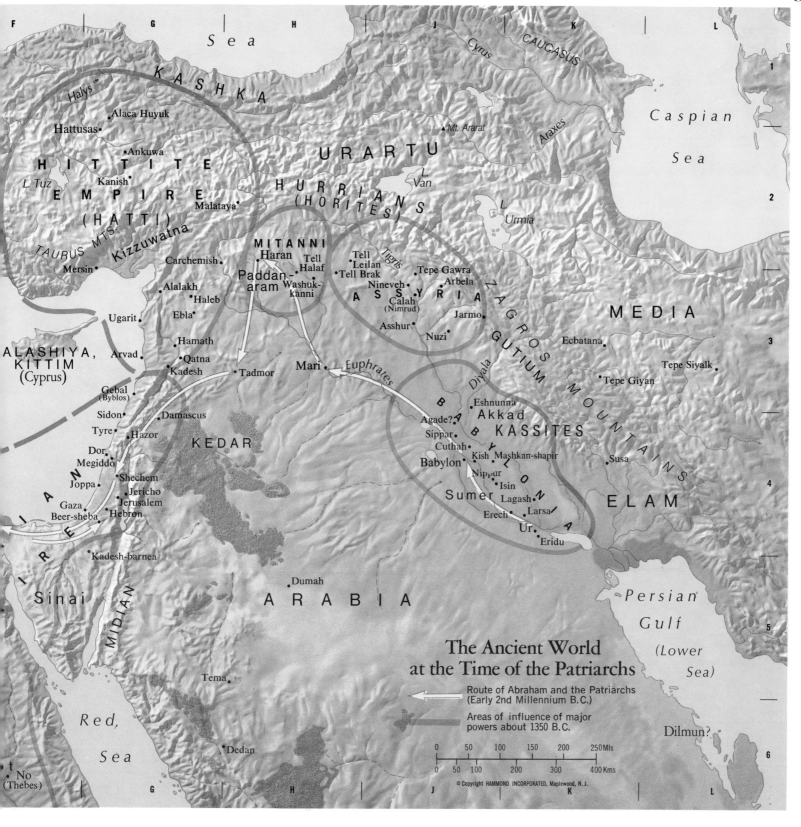

The Ancient World
at the Time of the Patriarchs

→ Route of Abraham and the Patriarchs
(Early 2nd Millennium B.C.)

━━ Areas of influence of major
powers about 1350 B.C.

```
0    50    100   150   200   250 Mls
0  50  100    200    300    400 Kms
```

© Copyright HAMMOND INCORPORATED, Maplewood, N.J.

In the royal tombs at Ur was found this magnificent sounding box of a lyre. The bull's head is of gold, silver and lapis lazuli. Below the head are panels of shell inlay.

The Canaanite altar for burnt offerings at Megiddo. This splendid "high place" was built in the Early Bronze Age and continued in use as late as the 19th century B.C., the time of the Hebrew Patriarchs.

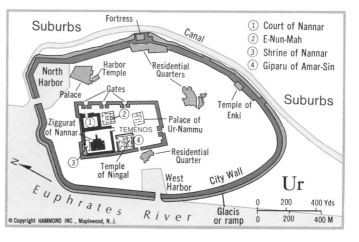

Suburbs — Fortress — Canal

① Court of Nannar
② E-Nun-Mah
③ Shrine of Nannar
④ Giparu of Amar-Sin

North Harbor — Harbor Temple — Palace — Residential Quarters — Gates — Ziggurat of Nannar — TEMENOS — Palace of Ur-Nammu — Temple of Enki — Suburbs — Temple of Ningal — Residential Quarter — West Harbor — City Wall

Ur

Euphrates River — Glacis or ramp

```
0    200    400 Yds
0   200   400 M
```

© Copyright HAMMOND INC., Maplewood, N.J.

In a timeless scene the pyramids dominate the sandy Egyptian horizon beyond the fertile fields of the Nile River plain.

A wall painting from the reign of Thutmoses III (15th century B.C.) shows the various stages of brickmaking.

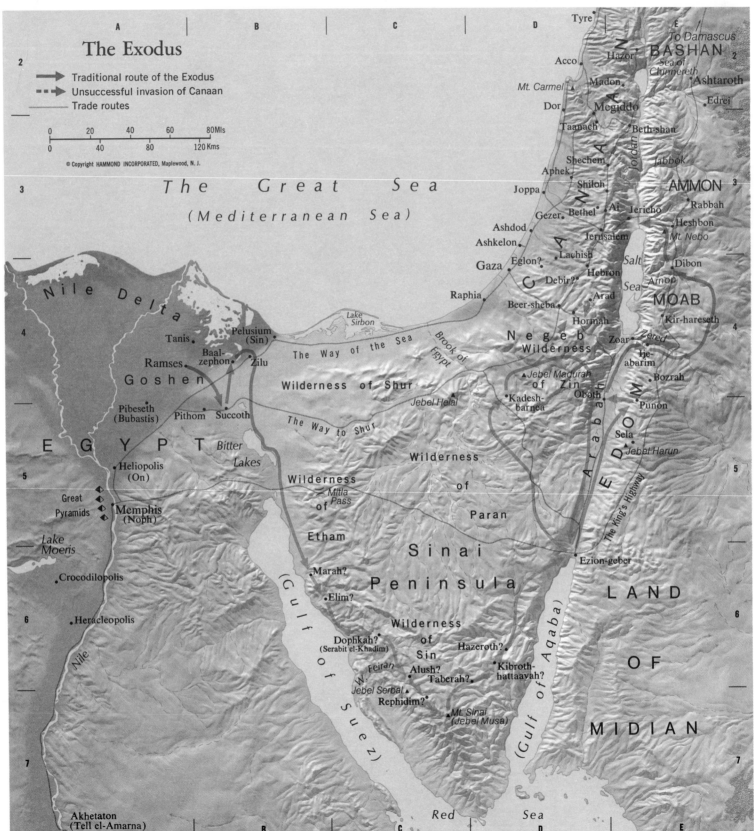

The Exodus

→ Traditional route of the Exodus
▶ Unsuccessful invasion of Canaan
— Trade routes

0 20 40 60 80Mls
0 40 80 120 Kms

© Copyright HAMMOND INCORPORATED, Maplewood, N.J.

The Great Sea
(Mediterranean Sea)

Nile Delta

Tanis
Baal-zephon
Zilu
Pelusium (Sin)
Ramses
Goshen
Pibeseth (Bubastis)
Pithom Succoth
Heliopolis (On)
Bitter Lakes
Great Pyramids
Memphis (Noph)
Lake Moeris
Crocodilopolis
Heracleopolis
Nile

EGYPT

The Way of the Sea
Wilderness of Shur
The Way to Shur
Lake Sirbon
Jebel Helal
Brook of Egypt
Kadesh-barnea
Wilderness of Paran
Wilderness of Etham
Marah?
Elim?
Wilderness of Sin
Dophkah? (Serabit el-Khadim)
W. Feiran
Jebel Serbal
Rephidim?
Alush? Taberah?
Hazeroth?
Kibroth-hattaavah?
Mt. Sinai (Jebel Musa)

Sinai Peninsula

(Gulf of Suez)
(Gulf of Aqaba)

Red Sea

Tyre
Acco
Hazor
Mt. Carmel
Dor
Taanach
Shechem
Aphek
Joppa
Gezer Bethel Ai Jericho
Ashdod
Ashkelon
Gaza Eglon?
Lachish
Debir?
Raphia
Beer-sheba
Hormah
Negeb Wilderness
Jebel Madurah
of Zin
Oboth
Sela
Jebel Harun

BASHAN
Sea of Chinnereth
Ashtaroth
Edrei
Beth-shan
Madon
Megiddo
Shiloh
AMMON
Rabbah
Heshbon
Jerusalem Mt. Nebo
Salt Sea
Hebron Dibon
Arad Arnon
MOAB
Kir-hareseth
Zoar Zered
Ije-abarim
Bozrah
Punon
EDOM
Arabah
The King's Highway
Ezion-geber

LAND OF MIDIAN

Akhetaton (Tell el-Amarna)

Mount Tabor, where the forces of Deborah gathered to give battle to the army of Sisera (Judges 4:6f.). A torrent turned the Esdraelon Plain in the foreground into a quagmire, rendering Sisera's Canaanite chariots ineffective.

Bronze figurine of a young bull found at a cult center on a hill near Mt. Ebal; circa 1200 B.C.

Early Israelite Settlement in Canaan

Area settled by Israelites

JUDAH Twelve Israelite tribes

Gezer Unconquered Canaanite city (according to Judges 1)

© Copyright HAMMOND INCORPORATED, Maplewood, N.J.

Sidon
Tyre
Ahlab
Beth-shemesh?
Dan (Laish)
Kedesh
Achzib
Merom
Beth-anath?
Hazor
Acco
Rehob
Aphek
Sea of Chinnereth
Ashtaroth
Golan
Shimron
Mt. Tabor
Edrei
Dor
Kishon
Jezreel
Havvoth-jair
Megiddo
Ramoth-gilead
Taanach
Beth-shan
Dothan
Ibleam
Jabesh-gilead
Hepher
Tirzah
Mt. Ebal
Shechem
Succoth
Mt. Gerizim
Jabbok
Aphek
Shiloh
Joppa
Bethel
Ai
Gilgal
Gath
Shaalbim
Gezer
Gibeon
Jericho
Aijalon
Ekron
Heshbon
Bezer
Ashdod
Jerusalem
Mt. Nebo
Libnah
Beth-shemesh
Ashkelon
Adullam
Gath?
Beth-zur
Gaza
Eglon?
Lachish
Hebron
Salt Sea
Aroer
Gerar
Debir?
Arnon
Ziklag?
Arad
Beer-sheba
MOAB
Hormah
Kir-hareseth
Zoar
Tamar
EDOM

The Great Sea

MT. LEBANON
MT. HERMON
Damascus
Bashan
Gilead
AMMON
Rabbah
Jazer
REUBEN
Negeb
SIMEON

0 5 10 15 20 25 30 35 Mls
0 10 20 30 40 50 60 Kms

Israel's Entry into Canaan
According to the Book of Joshua

Israelite campaigns
Canaanite campaigns

Shiloh
Gath (Gittaim)
Aijalon
Ascent of Beth-horon
Bethel
Beeroth
Ai
Gilgal
Jericho
Gezer
Aijalon
Chephirah
Kiriath-jearim
Gibeon
Ekron
Sorek
JEBUSITES
Jerusalem
Qumran (City of Salt)
Makkedah
Jarmuth
Libnah
Azekah
Adullam
Gath?
Beth-zur
Lachish
Eglon?
Hebron
Debir?
En-gedi

HIVITES
HITTITES
Salt Sea

0 5 10 15 Mls
0 5 10 15 20 25 Kms

© Copyright HAMMOND INC., Maplewood, N.J.

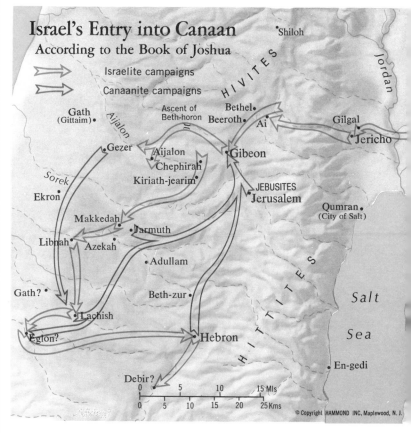

The fortress-temple of Baal-berith, probably the scene of Joshua's covenant (Joshua 9:4f.), was built at Shechem around 1650 B.C. and with modifications continued in use throughout the Period of the Judges.

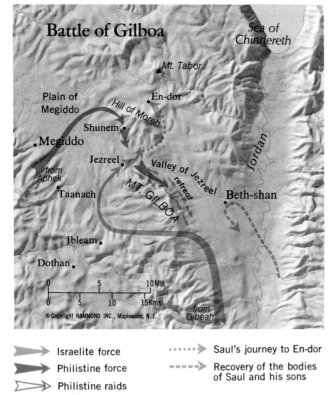

Battle of Gilboa

Sea of Chinnereth
Mt. Tabor
Plain of Megiddo
Hill of Moreh
En-dor
Shunem
Megiddo
Jezreel
from Aphek
Valley of Jezreel
retreat
Taanach
MT. GILBOA
Beth-shan
Ibleam
Dothan
Jordan

0 5 10Mls
0 5 10 15Kms
© Copyright HAMMOND INC., Maplewood, N.J.
from Gibeah

➡ Israelite force
➡ Philistine force
▷ Philistine raids
┈┈▹ Saul's journey to En-dor
┄┄▹ Recovery of the bodies of Saul and his sons

Battle of Michmash

Ophrah
Bethel
Lower Beth-horon
Upper Beth-horon
Michmash
Gilgal
Aijalon
retreat
Gibeon
Geba
Kiriath-jearim
Gibeah
to Geba
to Michmash
Jerusalem
Beth-shemesh
Bethlehem
Wilderness of Judah
Salt Sea

0 5 10 15Mls
0 5 10 15 20 25Kms
© Copyright HAMMOND INC., Maplewood, N.J.

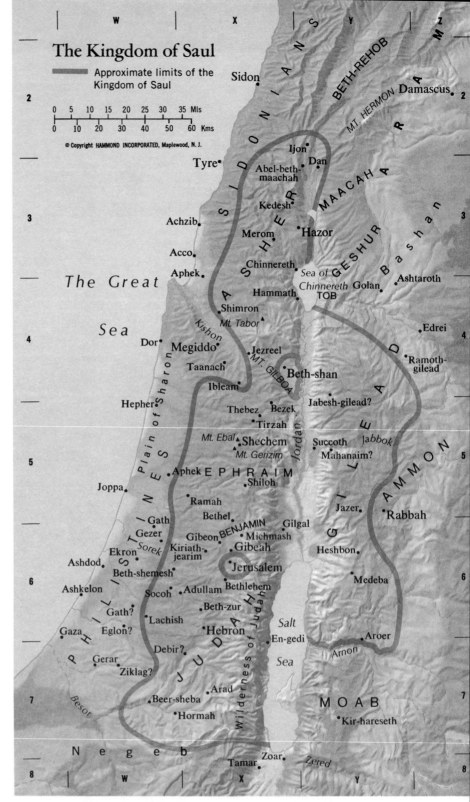

The Kingdom of Saul

━━━ Approximate limits of the Kingdom of Saul

0 5 10 15 20 25 30 35 Mls
0 10 20 30 40 50 60 Kms
© Copyright HAMMOND INCORPORATED, Maplewood, N.J.

W X Y Z

BETH-REHOB
Sidon
MT. HERMON
Damascus
Tyre
Ijon
Dan
Abel-beth-maachah
MAACAH
Kedesh
Achzib
Merom
Hazor
GESHUR
Bashan
Acco
Chinnereth
Aphek
Sea of Chinnereth
Golan
Ashtaroth
Hammath
TOB
The Great
Shimron
Mt. Tabor
Kishon
Edrei
Sea
Dor
Megiddo
Jezreel
MT. GILBOA
Ramoth-gilead
Taanach
Beth-shan
Ibleam
Jabesh-gilead?
Hepher
Thebez
Bezek
Tirzah
Mt. Ebal
Shechem
Succoth
Jabbok
Mt. Gerizim
Mahanaim?
AMMON
Aphek
EPHRAIM
Shiloh
Joppa
Ramah
Jazer
Rabbah
Gath
Bethel
Gezer
Gibeon
BENJAMIN
Gilgal
Michmash
Heshbon
Ekron
Sorek
Kiriath-jearim
Gibeah
Ashdod
Jerusalem
Medeba
Beth-shemesh
Ashkelon
Socoh
Adullam
Bethlehem
Salt
Gath?
Beth-zur
En-gedi
Sea
Gaza
Eglon?
Lachish
Hebron
Aroer
Debir?
Arnon
Gerar
Ziklag?
Arad
MOAB
Beer-sheba
Hormah
Kir-haresheth
N e g e b
Tamar
Zoar
Zered

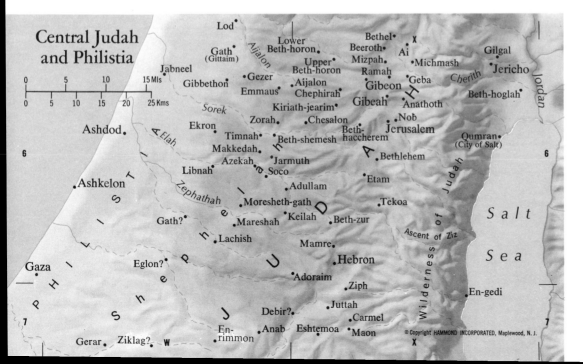

Central Judah and Philistia

0 5 10 15Mls
0 5 10 15 20 25 Kms

Lod
Bethel
Gath (Gittaim)
Lower Beth-horon
Beeroth
Ai
Gilgal
Jabneel
Upper Beth-horon
Mizpah
Michmash
Jericho
Gibbethon
Gezer
Emmaus
Aijalon
Chephirah
Ramah
Gibeon
Geba
Beth-hoglah
Kiriath-jearim
Gibeah
Anathoth
Sorek
Zorah
Chesalon
Nob
Ashdod
Ekron
Timnah
Beth-shemesh
Beth-haccherem
Jerusalem
Qumran (City of Salt)
Makkedah
Bethlehem
Azekah
Jarmuth
Libnah
Soco
Etam
Ashkelon
Adullam
Salt
Moresheth-gath
Tekoa
Sea
Gath?
Mareshah
Keilah
Beth-zur
Ascent of Ziz
Lachish
Mamre
Gaza
Eglon?
Adoraim
Hebron
Ziph
Gerar
Ziklag?
Debir?
Juttah
En-gedi
En-rimmon
Anab
Eshtemoa
Maon
Carmel
Wilderness of Judah

© Copyright HAMMOND INCORPORATED, Maplewood, N.J.

The rude remains of Saul's fortress-palace at Gibeah (background) surrounded by later construction (foreground) contrast sharply with the magnificence of Solomon's buildings.

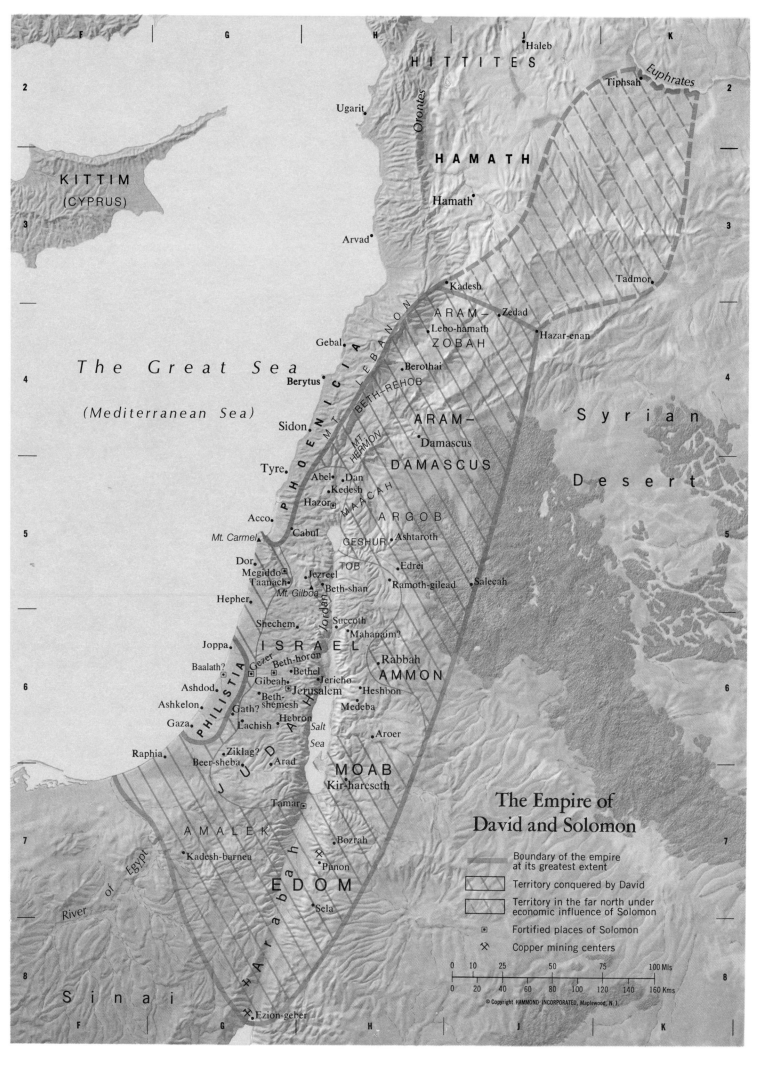

HITTITES

Haleb

Euphrates

Ugarit

Tiphsah

HAMATH

Orontes

KITTIM
(CYPRUS)

Hamath

Arvad

Tadmor

Kadesh

Zedad

ARAM –

Lebo-hamath

Hazar-enan

Gebal

ZOBAH

The Great Sea

Berothai

Berytus

BETH-REHOB

(Mediterranean Sea)

MT
HERMON

ARAM –

Sidon

Damascus

Tyre

DAMASCUS

Abel

Dan

Kedesh

Hazor

MAACAH

ARGOB

Acco

S y r i a n

Cabul

GESHUR

Ashtaroth

Mt. Carmel

TOB

Dor

Edrei

D e s e r t

Megiddo

Jezreel

Taanach

Ramoth-gilead

Salecah

Mt. Gilboa

Beth-shan

Hepher

Succoth

Shechem

Mahanaim?

Jordan

Joppa

ISRAEL

Baalath?

Gezer

Beth-horon

Rabbah

Bethel

Gibeah

AMMON

Ashdod

Jericho

Heshbon

Beth-

Jerusalem

Ashkelon

shemesh

PHILISTIA

Gath?

Medeba

Gaza

Lachish

Hebron

Salt

JUDAH

Sea

Raphia

Ziklag?

Arad

Aroer

Beer-sheba

MOAB

Tamar

Kir-hareseth

The Empire of
David and Solomon

AMALEK

River

Bozrah

Kadesh-barnea

Punon

of

————— Boundary of the empire
at its greatest extent

Egypt

Arabah

EDOM

Territory conquered by David

Sela

Territory in the far north under
economic influence of Solomon

⊡ Fortified places of Solomon

S i n a i

✕ Copper mining centers

0	10	25	50	75	100 Mls
0	20	40	60	80 100	120 140 160 Kms

Ezion-geber

© Copyright HAMMOND INCORPORATED, Maplewood, N.J.

14

Solomonic Gate
at Gezer

A proto-Ionic capital of the type that
graced the gates of the royal cities and
palaces of Israel and Judah: Samaria,
Megiddo, Hazor, Ramat Rahel and
most likely Jerusalem and Gezer.

The Israelite gate at Gezer is one of the finest
Solomonic structures yet found. Its design of
two outer towers and six flanking guardrooms
is virtually identical to Solomon's fortification
gates at Megiddo and Hazor.

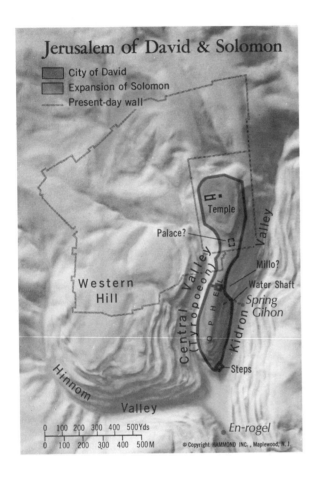

Jerusalem of David & Solomon

- City of David
- Expansion of Solomon
- Present-day wall

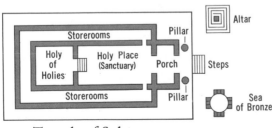

Temple of Solomon

Solomon's Twelve Districts

Boundary of tax districts
Gezer Royal City of Solomon
▣ Places fortified by Solomon

© Copyright HAMMOND INCORPORATED, Maplewood, N.J.

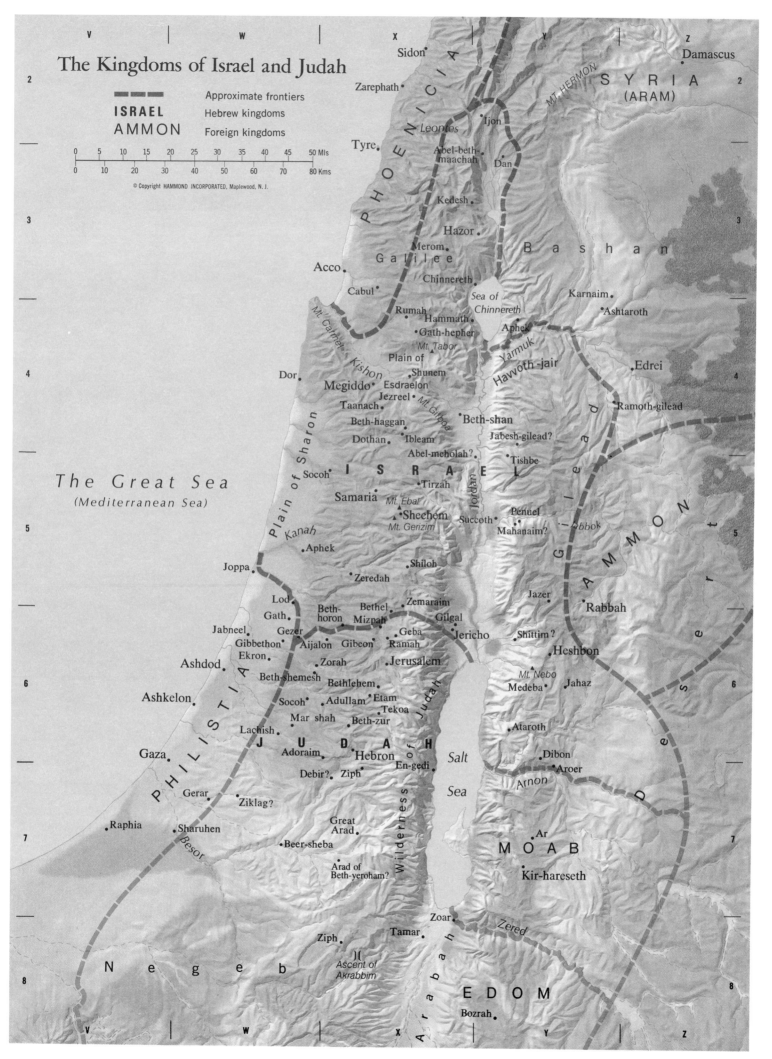

The Kingdoms of Israel and Judah

– – – – Approximate frontiers

ISRAEL Hebrew kingdoms

AMMON Foreign kingdoms

0 5 10 15 20 25 30 35 40 45 50 Mls
0 10 20 30 40 50 60 70 80 Kms

© Copyright HAMMOND INCORPORATED, Maplewood, N.J.

SYRIA (ARAM)

Damascus

Sidon

Zarephath

MT. HERMON

PHOENICIA

Leontes

Ijon

Tyre

Abel-beth-maachah

Dan

Kedesh

Hazor

Bashan

Merom

Galilee

Acco

Chinnereth

Cabul

Sea of Chinnereth

Karnaim

Rumah

Ashtaroth

Hammath

Gath-hepher

Aphek

Mt. Carmel

Kishon

Mt. Tabor

Yarmuk

Edrei

Plain of

Havvoth-jair

Dor

Shunem

Megiddo

Esdraelon

Jezreel

Mt. Gilboa

Ramoth-gilead

Taanach

Beth-haggan

Beth-shan

Jabesh-gilead?

Dothan

Ibleam

Abel-meholah?

Tishbe

Plain of Sharon

Socoh

ISRAEL

Tirzah

Jordan

The Great Sea

(Mediterranean Sea)

Samaria

Mt. Ebal

Shechem

Mt. Gerizim

Succoth

Penuel

Mahanaim?

Jabbok

Kanah

Aphek

Shiloh

Joppa

Zeredah

AMMON

Jazer

Rabbah

Lod

Zemaraim

Gath

Beth-horon

Bethel

Mizpah

Gilgal

Jabneel

Gezer

Geba

Jericho

Shittim?

Gibbethon

Aijalon

Gibeon

Ramah

Heshbon

Ekron

Zorah

Jerusalem

Ashdod

Mt. Nebo

Beth-shemesh

Bethlehem

Medeba

Jahaz

Ashkelon

Socoh

Adullam

Etam

Mar shah

Tekoa

Beth-zur

Ataroth

Lachish

Wilderness of Judah

JUDAH

Gaza

Adoraim

Hebron

Salt

Dibon

Aroer

Debir?

Ziph

En-gedi

Sea

Arnon

Gerar

Ziklag?

MOAB

Raphia

Sharuhen

Great Arad

Ar

Besor

Beer-sheba

Kir-hareseth

Arad of Beth-yeroham?

Zoar

Ziph

Tamar

Zered

Arabah

Negeb

Ascent of Akrabbim

EDOM

Bozrah

Gilead

Desert

PHILISTIA

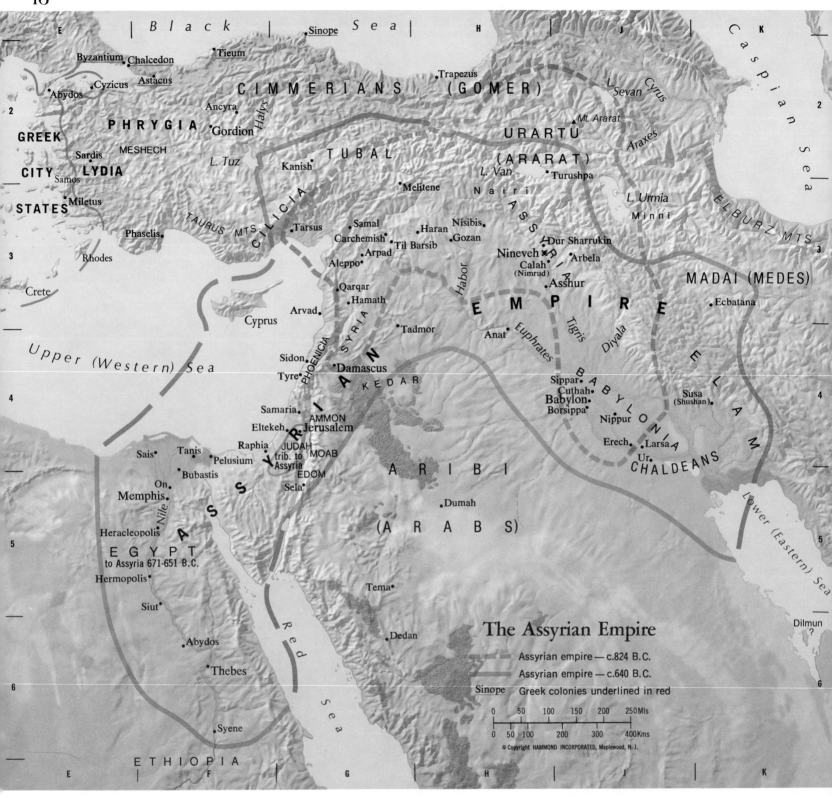

The Assyrian Empire

Assyrian empire — c.824 B.C.

Assyrian empire — c.640 B.C.

Sinope   Greek colonies underlined in red

0   50   100   150   200   250 Mls

0   50 100   200   300   400 Kms

© Copyright HAMMOND INCORPORATED, Maplewood, N.J.

Tiglath-pileser III extended the Assyrian Empire in the 8th century B.C. and caused political chaos in Israel.

The only contemporary picture of a Hebrew monarch occurs on the Black Obelisk, an Assyrian monument from Nimrud. It shows Jehu, on his knees before Shalmaneser III.

Assyrian wall relief from the throne room of Sennacherib shows Hebrews fleeing the doomed city of Lachish in southwest Judah when it was under Assyrian siege in 701 B.C.

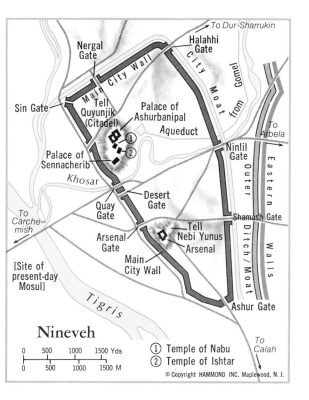

Nineveh

Nergal Gate
Halahhi Gate
Sin Gate
City Wall
City Wall
To Dur-Sharrukin
Main City Wall
Tell Quyunjik (Citadel)
Palace of Ashurbanipal
Aqueduct
Palace of Sennacherib
Khosar
Ninlil Gate
To Arbela
Outer Ditch/Moat
Eastern Walls
Gomel from
To Carche-mish
Desert Gate
Quay Gate
Arsenal Gate
Tell Nebi Yunus
Arsenal
Main City Wall
Shamash Gate
[Site of present-day Mosul]
Tigris
Ashur Gate
To Calah

① Temple of Nabu
② Temple of Ishtar

| 0 | 500 | 1000 | 1500 Yds |
| 0 | 500 | 1000 | 1500 M |

© Copyright HAMMOND INC. Maplewood, N.J.

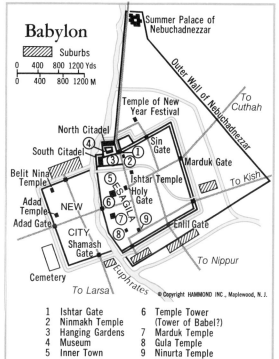

Babylon

⧅ Suburbs

| 0 | 400 | 800 | 1200 Yds |
| 0 | 400 | 800 | 1200 M |

Summer Palace of Nebuchadnezzar
Outer Wall of Nebuchadnezzar
To Cuthah
Temple of New Year Festival
North Citadel
South Citadel
Sin Gate
Marduk Gate
Belit Nina Temple
Ishtar Temple
To Kish
Adad Temple
ESAGILA
Holy Gate
Enlil Gate
Adad Gate
NEW CITY
Shamash Gate
To Nippur
Cemetery
Euphrates
To Larsa

© Copyright HAMMOND INC., Maplewood, N.J.

1 Ishtar Gate
2 Ninmakh Temple
3 Hanging Gardens
4 Museum
5 Inner Town
6 Temple Tower (Tower of Babel?)
7 Marduk Temple
8 Gula Temple
9 Ninurta Temple

A reconstruction of the Ishtar Gate at Babylon, with the famous "hanging gardens" in the right background. The king entering the gate is Nebuchadnezzar II (605-562 B.C.), who destroyed Jerusalem.

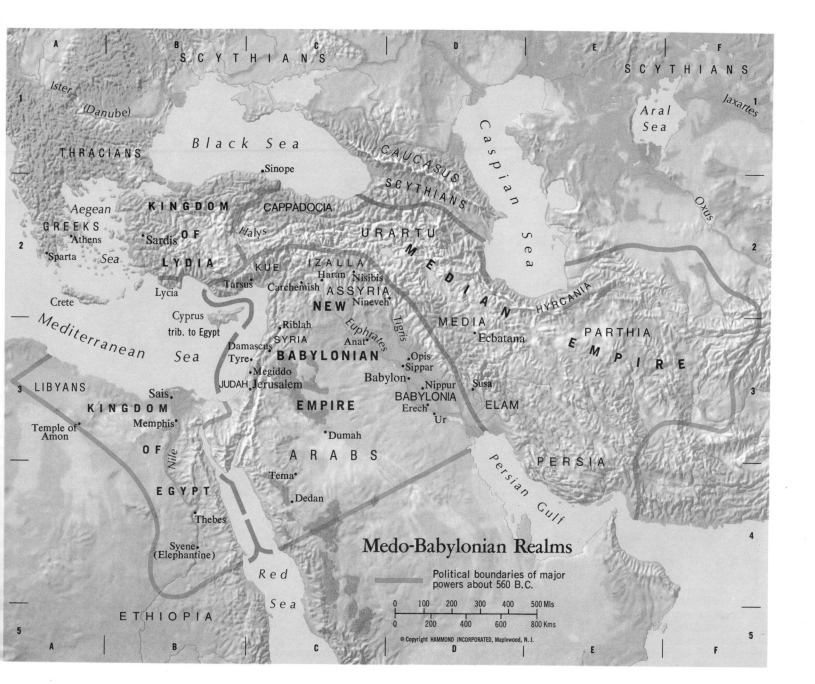

Medo-Babylonian Realms

— Political boundaries of major powers about 560 B.C.

| 0 | 100 | 200 | 300 | 400 | 500 Mls |
| 0 | 200 | 400 | 600 | 800 Kms |

© Copyright HAMMOND INCORPORATED, Maplewood, N.J.

SCYTHIANS
SCYTHIANS
Ister (Danube)
Aral Sea
Jaxartes
THRACIANS
Black Sea
Sinope
CAUCASUS
SCYTHIANS
Caspian Sea
Oxus
Aegean Sea
GREEKS
Athens
Sparta
KINGDOM OF LYDIA
Sardis
CAPPADOCIA
Halys
URARTU
MEDIAN
HYRCANIA
KUE
IZALLA
Haran
Nisibis
Tarsus
Carchemish
ASSYRIA
Nineveh
Lycia
Crete
Cyprus
trib. to Egypt
NEW
MEDIA
PARTHIA
EMPIRE
Mediterranean Sea
Riblah
SYRIA
Anat
Ecbatana
Damascus
Tyre
BABYLONIAN
Opis
Sippar
Megiddo
JUDAH Jerusalem
Babylon
Nippur
Susa
LIBYANS
EMPIRE
BABYLONIA
Erech
ELAM
KINGDOM OF
Sais
Ur
Temple of Amon
Memphis
Dumah
ARABS
PERSIA
EGYPT
Nile
Tema
Persian Gulf
Red Sea
Dedan
Thebes
Syene (Elephantine)
ETHIOPIA

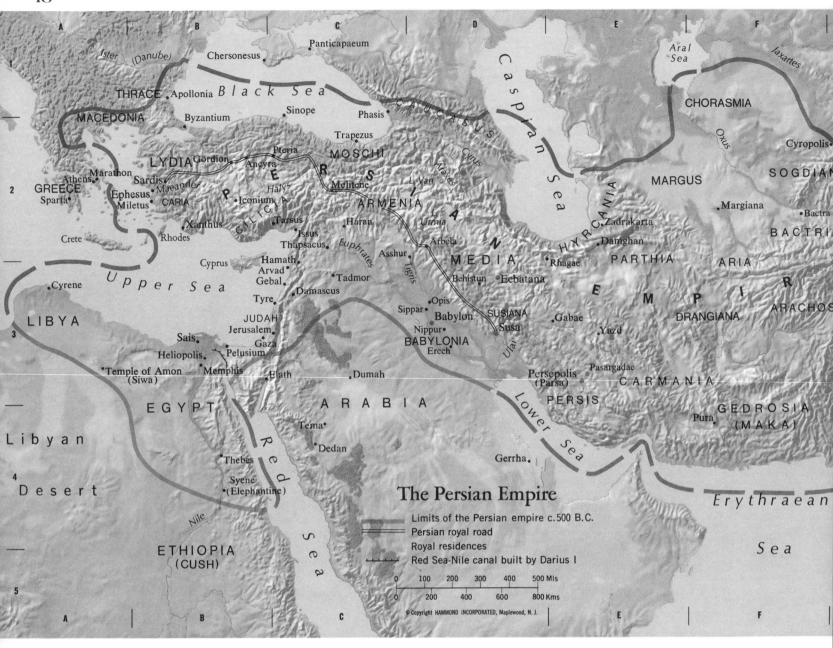

The Persian Empire

Limits of the Persian empire c.500 B.C.
Persian royal road
Royal residences
Red Sea-Nile canal built by Darius I

| 0 | 100 | 200 | 300 | 400 | 500 Mls |
| 0 | 200 | 400 | 600 | 800 Kms |

© Copyright HAMMOND INCORPORATED, Maplewood, N.J.

On this clay cylinder of 538 B.C., Cyrus provides royal authorization for the rebuilding of temples "beyond the Euphrates."

Tomb of Cyrus the Great at Pasargadae, Iran. When he conquered Babylon, Cyrus allowed the Jews to return to Jerusalem and rebuild their temple.

The earliest coin used in the Holy Land is this 4th-century silver Persian piece. The obverse has a falcon with the inscription "Yahud." The reverse has a lily with no inscription.

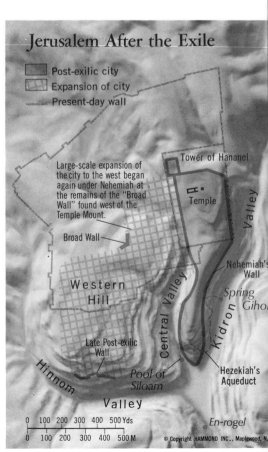

Jerusalem After the Exile

Post-exilic city
Expansion of city
Present-day wall

Large-scale expansion of the city to the west began again under Nehemiah at the remains of the "Broad Wall" found west of the Temple Mount.

Broad Wall

Tower of Hananel

Temple

Nehemiah's Wall

Western Hill

Spring Gihon

Late Post-exilic Wall

Pool of Siloam

Hezekiah's Aqueduct

Hinnom Valley

Central Valley

Kidron Valley

En-rogel

| 0 | 100 | 200 | 300 | 400 | 500 Yds |
| 0 | 100 | 200 | 300 | 400 | 500 M |

© Copyright HAMMOND INC., Maplewood, N.

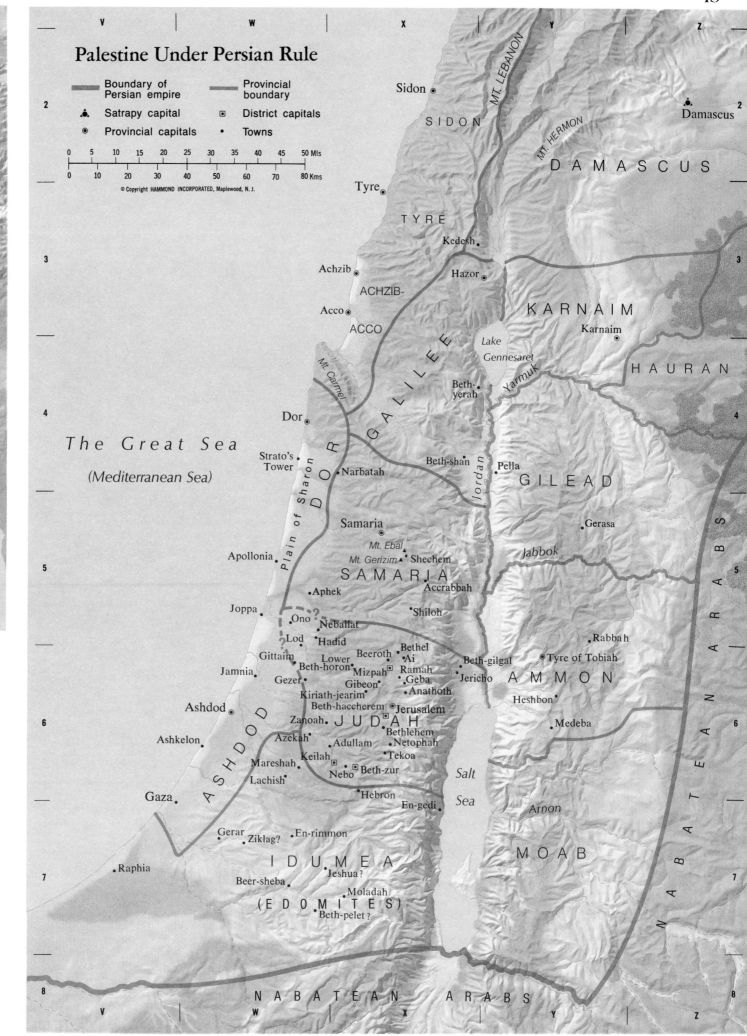

Palestine Under Persian Rule

Boundary of Persian empire
Provincial boundary
Satrapy capital
District capitals
Provincial capitals
Towns

0 5 10 15 20 25 30 35 40 45 50 Mls
0 10 20 30 40 50 60 70 80 Kms

© Copyright HAMMOND INCORPORATED, Maplewood, N.J.

**(SCYTHIANS
SAKA)**

HINDU KUSH

Cophen
(Kabul)
Taxila

GANDARA

HINDUSH
(INDIA)

Pattala

Probable
ancient
coastline

Sidon

SIDON

MT. LEBANON

MT. HERMON

Damascus

DAMASCUS

Tyre

TYRE

Kedesh

Achzib

ACHZIB-

Hazor

KARNAIM

Karnaim

HAURAN

Acco

ACCO

The Great Sea

(Mediterranean Sea)

Mt. Carmel

GALILEE

Lake
Gennesaret

Beth-
yerah

Yarmuk

Dor

DOR

Strato's
Tower

Narbatah

Beth-shan

Pella

Jordan

GILEAD

Gerasa

Plain of Sharon

Samaria

Mt. Ebal
Mt. Gerizim ▲ Shechem

Jabbok

Apollonia

SAMARIA

Aphek

Accrabbah

Joppa

Ono

Neballat

Shiloh

Rabbah

Lod

Hadid

Bethel
Ai

Beth-gilgal

Tyre of Tobiah

Gittaim

Lower
Beth-horon

Beeroth

Mizpah

Ramah

Geba

Jericho

AMMON

Jamnia

Gezer

Gibeon

Anathoth

Kiriath-jearim

Heshbon

Ashdod

Beth-haccerem

Jerusalem

Zanoah

JUDAH

Bethlehem

Medeba

ASHDOD

Azekah

Adullam

Netophah

Ashkelon

Keilah

Tekoa

Mareshah

Nebo

Beth-zur

Salt

Lachish

Sea

Gaza

Hebron

En-gedi

Arnon

Gerar

Ziklag?

En-rimmon

MOAB

Raphia

IDUMEA

Jeshua?

Beer-sheba

Moladah

(EDOMITES)

Beth-pelet?

NABATEAN ARABS

NABATEAN ARABS

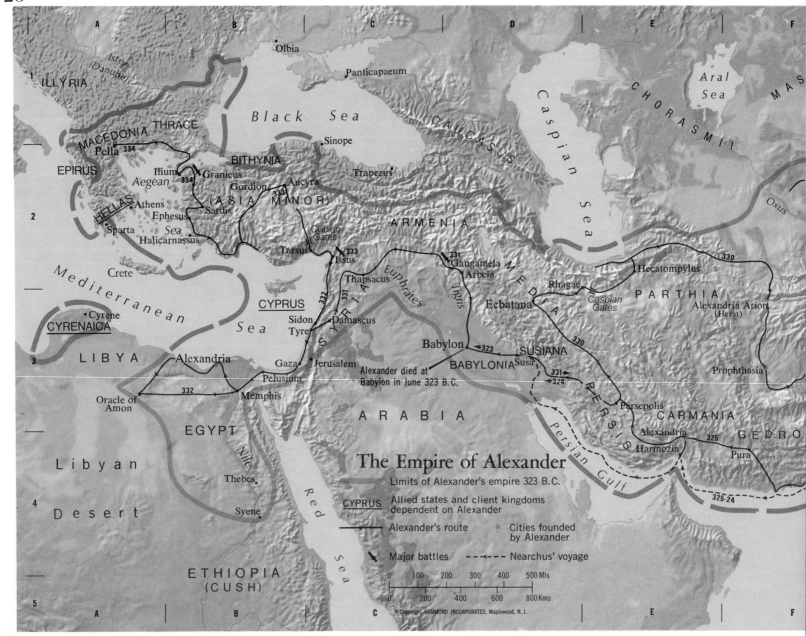

The Empire of Alexander

Limits of Alexander's empire 323 B.C.

<u>CYPRUS</u> Allied states and client kingdoms dependent on Alexander

Alexander's route   • Cities founded by Alexander

↖ Major battles   -·-·- Nearchus' voyage

| 0 | 100 | 200 | 300 | 400 | 500 Mls |
| 0 | 200 | | 400 | 600 | 800 Kms |

© Copyright HAMMOND INCORPORATED, Maplewood, N.J.

Alexander died at Babylon in June 323 B.C.

Alexander the Great at the Battle of Issus, where he defeated the Persians. This Roman mosaic from Pompeii shows the determination of this brilliant soldier who established an empire at age thirty.

Silver tetradrachm of Ptolemy I struck in Egypt shows Alexander wearing an elephant headdress. Reverse: the goddess Athena.

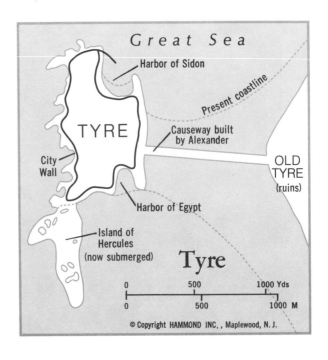

Great Sea

Harbor of Sidon

Present coastline

TYRE

Causeway built by Alexander

City Wall

OLD TYRE (ruins)

Harbor of Egypt

Island of Hercules (now submerged)

Tyre

| 0 | 500 | 1000 Yds |
| 0 | 500 | 1000 M |

© Copyright HAMMOND INC., Maplewood, N.J.

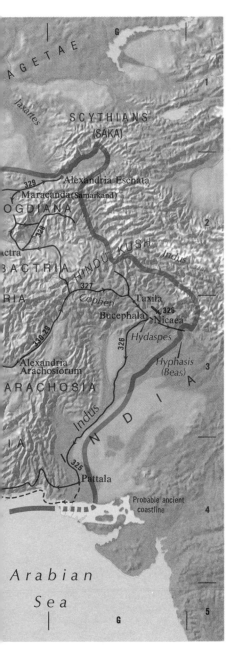

Massive round towers such as this one were set into Israelite walls at Samaria by Alexander's military engineers. Samaria, once capital of Israel, became one of the most Hellenized cities of Palestine.

Seleucus I, "Nicator," continued Alexander's Hellenizing policies.

Ptolemy I, "Soter," turned Egypt into his personal domain.

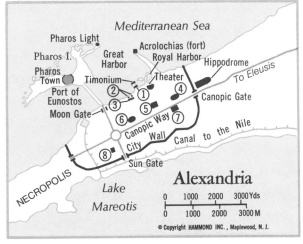

Alexandria

Mediterranean Sea

Pharos Light
Pharos I.
Pharos Town
Port of Eunostos
Moon Gate
Great Harbor
Timonium
Acrolochias (fort)
Royal Harbor
Theater
Hippodrome
To Eleusis
Canopic Gate
Canopic Way
City Wall
Canal to the Nile
Sun Gate

NECROPOLIS

Lake Mareotis

| 0 | 1000 | 2000 | 3000 Yds |
| 0 | 1000 | 2000 | 3000 M |

© Copyright HAMMOND INC., Maplewood, N.J.

1 Poseidium
2 Obelisks (later Cleopatra's Needles)
3 Caesarium
4 Stadium
5 Library and Museum
6 Amphitheater
7 Sports Grounds
8 Serapeion

Terracotta statuette of a war elephant with driver and tower.

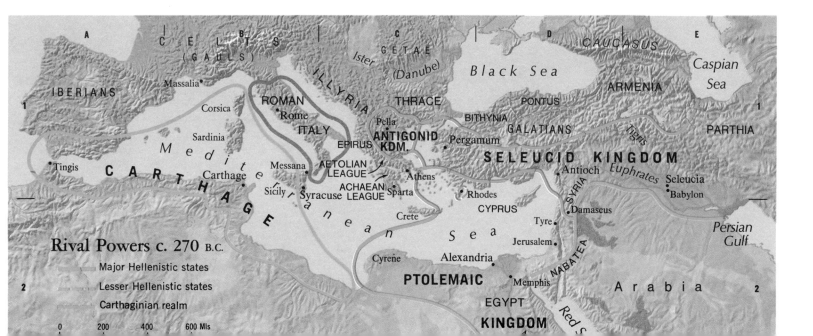

Rival Powers c. 270 B.C.

Major Hellenistic states
Lesser Hellenistic states
Carthaginian realm

| 0 | 200 | 400 | 600 Mls |

CELTS (GAULS)
IBERIANS
Massalia
Corsica
ROMAN
Rome
ITALY
Sardinia
Tingis
CARTHAGE
Carthage
Sicily
Messana
Syracuse
EPIRUS
ILLYRIA
Ister (Danube)
GETAE
THRACE
Pella
ANTIGONID KDM.
AETOLIAN LEAGUE
ACHAEAN LEAGUE
Athens
Sparta
Crete
Mediterranean Sea
Black Sea
CAUCASUS
Caspian Sea
ARMENIA
PONTUS
BITHYNIA
GALATIANS
Pergamum
SELEUCID KINGDOM
PARTHIA
Antioch
Euphrates
Tigris
Seleucia
Babylon
Damascus
SYRIA
Tyre
Rhodes
CYPRUS
Jerusalem
NABATEA
Cyrene
Alexandria
PTOLEMAIC
Memphis
Arabia
EGYPT
KINGDOM
Persian Gulf
Red S.

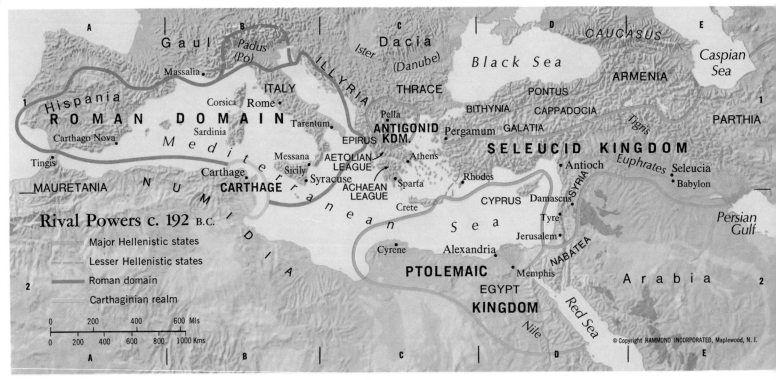

Rival Powers c. 192 B.C.

- Major Hellenistic states
- Lesser Hellenistic states
- Roman domain
- Carthaginian realm

Antiochus III, "The Great," who took Palestine from the Ptolemies at the Battle of Panias in 197 B.C.

Naked Greek youths participating in athletic contests are pictured on this 6th-century B.C. Greek vase. Such practices introduced into Jerusalem were a cause of the Maccabean Revolt.

Jerusalem of the Maccabees

- Maximum extent of Maccabean city
- Wall alignment uncertain
- Present-day wall

Antiochus IV, "Epiphanes," tried to Hellenize the Jews, which led to the Maccabean War in 166 B.C.

A lepton of Alexander Jannaeus (103-76 B.C.), who expanded the Jewish Hasmonean Kingdom to its greatest limits. This coin is popularly known as the "widow's mite" of the New Testament.

Antigonus II (40-37 B.C.), the last of the Hasmonean rulers, issued

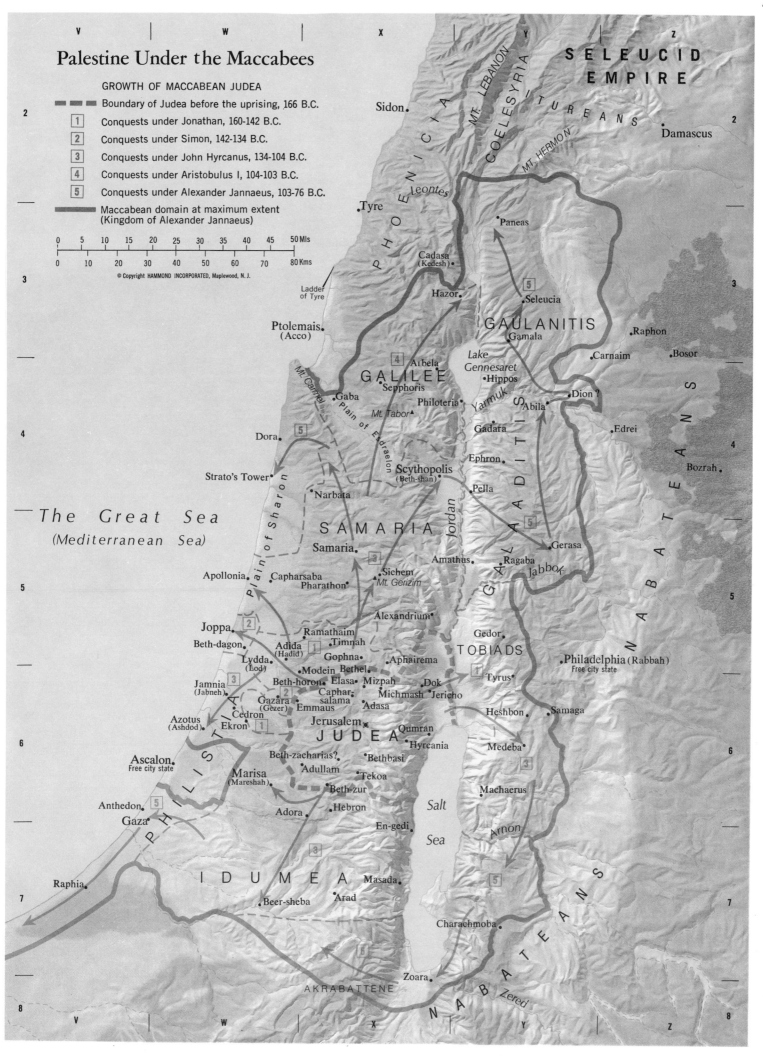

Palestine Under the Maccabees

GROWTH OF MACCABEAN JUDEA

- – – Boundary of Judea before the uprising, 166 B.C.
- 1 Conquests under Jonathan, 160-142 B.C.
- 2 Conquests under Simon, 142-134 B.C.
- 3 Conquests under John Hyrcanus, 134-104 B.C.
- 4 Conquests under Aristobulus I, 104-103 B.C.
- 5 Conquests under Alexander Jannaeus, 103-76 B.C.
- —— Maccabean domain at maximum extent (Kingdom of Alexander Jannaeus)

0 5 10 15 20 25 30 35 40 45 50 Mls
0 10 20 30 40 50 60 70 80 Kms

© Copyright HAMMOND INCORPORATED, Maplewood, N.J.

SELEUCID EMPIRE

The Great Sea (Mediterranean Sea)

Salt Sea

Sidon · Damascus · Tyre · Ptolemais (Acco) · Hazor · Seleucia · GAULANITIS · Gamala · Paneas · Raphon · Bosor · Carnaim · GALILEE · Sepphoris · Arbela · Lake Gennesaret · Hippos · Dion? · Abila · Edrei · Gadara · Bozrah · Ephron · Pella · Scythopolis (Beth-shan) · Gerasa · Dora · Strato's Tower · Narbata · SAMARIA · Samaria · Sichem · Amathus · Ragaba · Apollonia · Capharsaba · Pharathon · Alexandrium · Gedor · Philadelphia (Rabbah) · Joppa · Ramathaim · Timnah · TOBIADS · Tyrus · Beth-dagon · Adida (Hadid) · Gophna · Aphairema · Lydda (Lod) · Modein · Bethel · Beth-horon · Elasa · Mizpah · Dok · Heshbon · Samaga · Jamnia (Jabneh) · Caphar-salama · Michmash · Jericho · Gazara (Gezer) · Emmaus · Adasa · Azotus (Ashdod) · Cedron · Ekron · Jerusalem · Qumran · Medeba · JUDEA · Hyrcania · Ascalon · Beth-zacharias? · Bethbasi · Machaerus · Marisa (Mareshah) · Adullam · Tekoa · Beth-zur · Gaza · Adora · Hebron · En-gedi · Anthedon · Raphia · IDUMEA · Masada · Beer-sheba · Arad · Charachmoba · Zoara · AKRABATTENE · NABATEANS · GALAADITIS · PHOENICIA · COELESYRIA · ITUREANS · Mt. Hermon · Mt. Lebanon · PHILISTIA

The Roman World

Limits of direct Roman rule or political influence at the birth of Christ

Provincial or state boundaries

SYRIA   Roman provinces

<u>LYCIA</u>   Client kingdoms or states

| 0 | 100 | 200 | 300 | 400 | 500 Mls |
| 0 | 200 | 400 | 600 | 800 Kms |

© Copyright HAMMOND INCORPORATED, Maplewood, N.J.

Senate House in the Imperial Forum.

Octavian (Caesar-Augustus).

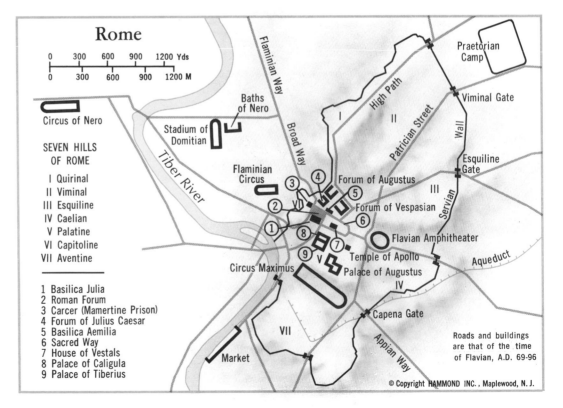

Rome

| 0 | 300 | 600 | 900 | 1200 Yds |
| 0 | 300 | 600 | 900 | 1200 M |

Circus of Nero

SEVEN HILLS OF ROME

I Quirinal
II Viminal
III Esquiline
IV Caelian
V Palatine
VI Capitoline
VII Aventine

1 Basilica Julia
2 Roman Forum
3 Carcer (Mamertine Prison)
4 Forum of Julius Caesar
5 Basilica Aemilia
6 Sacred Way
7 House of Vestals
8 Palace of Caligula
9 Palace of Tiberius

Roads and buildings are that of the time of Flavian, A.D. 69-96

© Copyright HAMMOND INC., Maplewood, N.J.

The Kingdom of Herod the Great

Boundary of Herod's kingdom
Other boundaries
▣ Cities of the Decapolis
⋈ Fortresses

0 5 10 15 20 25 30 35 40 45 50 Mls
0 10 20 30 40 50 60 70 80 Kms
© Copyright HAMMOND INCORPORATED, Maplewood, N.J.

Rha (Volga)

Caspian Sea

CAUCASUS
Iberia Albania
Colchis
ARMENIA
• Artaxata

PARTHIAN EMPIRE

Tigris
Euphrates
• Ctesiphon

Arabia

Mediterranean Sea

Chalcis
ABILENE
• Abila
Sidon
Phoenicia
MT. LEBANON
SYRIA
Iturea Damascus ▣
Leontes
Paneas
Tyre •
• Paneas
Ulatha
Cadasa •
Gischala •
Gaulanitis
Trachonitis
Batanea
Ptolemais •
GALILEE
• Bethsaida
▣ Raphana
Taricheae (Magdala) •
Sea of Galilee
Mt. Carmel
Gabae ⋈
• Sephoris
☐ Hippos
Auranitis
• Nazareth
▣ Dion ?
Dora •
Gadara ▣
Caesarea (Strato's Tower)
Scythopolis ▣
Bostra •
• Narbata
Pella ▣
DECAPOLIS
Plain of Sharon
SAMARIA
Gerasa ▣
Sebaste (Samaria) •
Apollonia •
Mt. Gerizim ▲
Amathus ⋈
Jordan
Jabbok
• Antipatris
Alexandrium ⋈
Joppa •
Phasaelis •
Gadara •
Philadelphia ▣
• Gophna
PEREA
Lydda •
Jamnia •
• Emmaus
Jericho •
Betharamphtha •
• Azotus
Cyprus ⋈
Esbus •
Jerusalem • • Bethany
Qumran •
Ascalon (free city)
Bethlehem •
Hyrcania ⋈
• Medeba
Agrippias (Anthedon)
• Herodium ⋈
Callirrhoe •
JUDEA
• Gaza
• Hebron
Machaerus ⋈
Adora •
Engaddi •
Lake Asphaltitis (Dead Sea)
Arnon
IDUMEA
Masada ⋈
• Bersabe
Malatha ⋈
NABATEA
• Elusa
Khirbet Tannur
Nabatean sanctuary
• Nessana

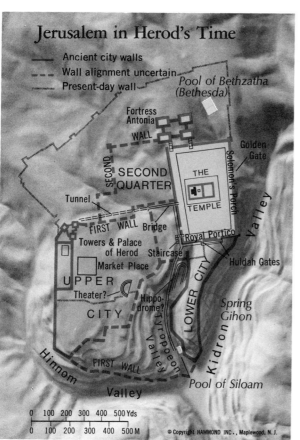

Jerusalem in Herod's Time

— Ancient city walls
-- Wall alignment uncertain
--- Present-day wall

Pool of Bethzatha (Bethesda)
Fortress Antonia
WALL
SECOND QUARTER
Golden Gate
Tunnel
SECOND
THE TEMPLE
Solomon's Porch
FIRST WALL
Bridge
Royal Portico
Towers & Palace of Herod
Staircase
Market Place
Huldah Gates
UPPER
Theater?
Hippodrome?
Spring Gihon
CITY
Tyropoeon Valley
LOWER CITY
Hinnom
FIRST WALL
Kidron Valley
Valley
Pool of Siloam

0 100 200 300 400 500 Yds
0 100 200 300 400 500 M
© Copyright HAMMOND INC., Maplewood, N.J.

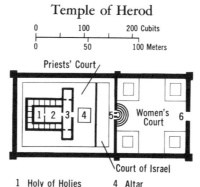

Temple of Herod

0 100 200 Cubits
0 50 100 Meters

Priests' Court
Women's Court
Court of Israel

1 Holy of Holies
2 Holy Place
3 Porch
4 Altar
5 Nicanor Gate
6 Beautiful Gate?

Model of Herod's Temple, with surrounding courts and Royal Portico in the background.

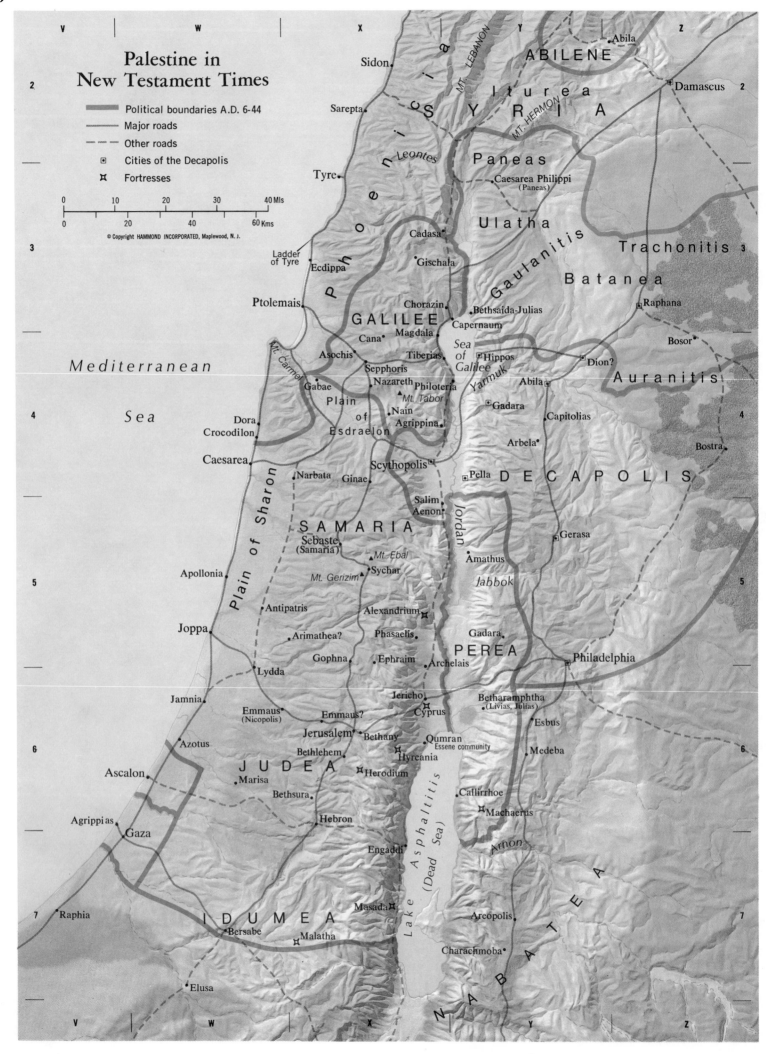

26

Palestine in New Testament Times

Political boundaries A.D. 6-44
Major roads
Other roads
▣ Cities of the Decapolis
⌘ Fortresses

0   10   20   30   40 Mls
0   20   40   60 Kms
© Copyright HAMMOND INCORPORATED, Maplewood, N.J.

Mediterranean

Sea

ABILENE

Sidon

SYRIA

Iturea

Abila

Damascus

Sarepta

MT. LEBANON

MT. HERMON

Paneas

Tyre

Leontes

Caesarea Philippi
(Paneas)

Ladder
of Tyre

Ulatha

Trachonitis

Ecdippa

Cadasa

Gischala

Batanea

Ptolemais

Chorazin

Bethsaida-Julias

Raphana

GALILEE

Capernaum

Bosor

Cana

Magdala

Asochis

Tiberias

Sea
of
Galilee

Hippos

Dion?

Aurenitis

Sepphoris

Nazareth

Philoteria

Yarmuk

Abila

Gabae

Mt. Tabor

Gadara

Plain

of

Nain

Capitolias

Dora

Esdraelon

Agrippina

Arbela

Crocodilon

Bostra

Scythopolis

Caesarea

Pella

DECAPOLIS

Narbata

Ginae

Salim
Aenon

Apollonia

SAMARIA

Jordan

Amathus

Sebaste
(Samaria)

Gerasa

Mt. Ebal

Antipatris

Mt. Gerizim

Sychar

Jabbok

Joppa

Alexandrium

Gadara

Arimathea?

Phasaelis

PEREA

Gophna

Ephraim

Archelais

Philadelphia

Lydda

Jamnia

Jericho

Betharamphtha
(Livias, Julias)

Emmaus
(Nicopolis)

Emmaus?

Cyprus

Esbus

Jerusalem

Bethany

Qumran
Essene community

Medeba

Azotus

Bethlehem

Hyrcania

Ascalon

JUDEA

Herodium

Callirrhoe

Marisa

Machaerus

Bethsura

Agrippias

Hebron

Gaza

Engaddi

Lake

Arnon

Raphia

IDUMEA

Masada

Areopolis

Bersabe

Malatha

Charachmoba

Elusa

NABATEA

Asphaltitis
(Dead Sea)

Plain of Sharon

Mt. Carmel

Phoenicia

Gaulanitis

26

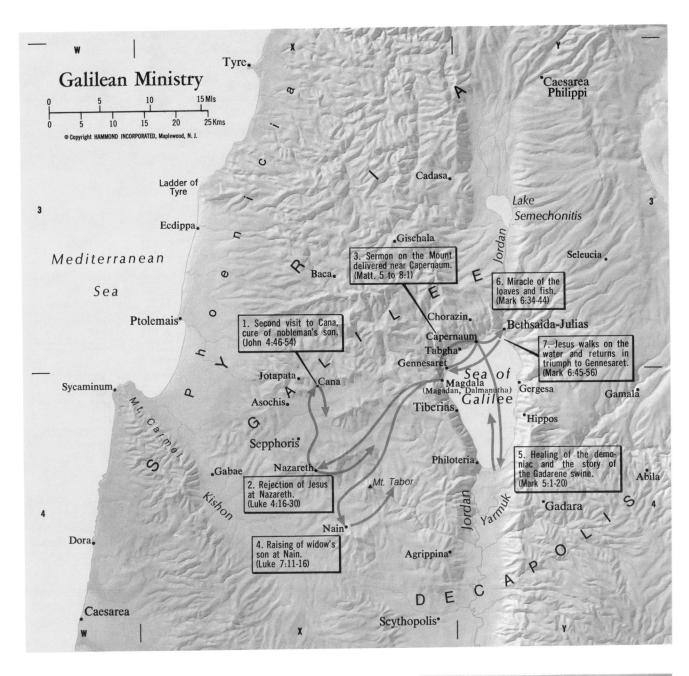

Galilean Ministry

0 5 10 15 Mls
0 5 10 15 20 25 Kms
© Copyright HAMMOND INCORPORATED, Maplewood, N.J.

W

Tyre.

Caesarea Philippi

Cadasa.

Lake Semechonitis

Mediterranean Sea

Ladder of Tyre

Ecdippa.

Gischala.

Seleucia.

3. Sermon on the Mount delivered near Capernaum. (Matt. 5 to 8:1)

6. Miracle of the loaves and fish. (Mark 6:34-44)

Baca.

Ptolemais•

1. Second visit to Cana, cure of nobleman's son. (John 4:46-54)

Chorazin.
Capernaum
Tabgha•
Gennesaret

Bethsaida-Julias

7. Jesus walks on the water and returns in triumph to Gennesaret. (Mark 6:45-56)

Sycaminum•

Jotapata•

Cana

Magdala
(Magadan, Dalmanutha)

Sea of Galilee

Gergesa

Gamala

Asochis.

Tiberias•

Hippos•

Sepphoris•

Philoteria•

5. Healing of the demoniac and the story of the Gadarene swine. (Mark 5:1-20)

Abila•

Gabae•

Nazareth•

2. Rejection of Jesus at Nazareth. (Luke 4:16-30)

Mt. Tabor

Gadara•

Dora.

Nain•

4. Raising of widow's son at Nain. (Luke 7:11-16)

Agrippina•

Caesarea

Scythopolis•

DECAPOLIS

Above the waters of the Sea of Galilee the Church of the Beatitudes dominates the hill where tradition says Jesus preached the Sermon on the Mount.

The excavated synagogue at Capernaum (right) is later than the time of Jesus, but recalls that the Galilean Ministry was based in Capernaum, where Jesus spent much time teaching and healing in the synagogue.

The River Jordan near the Dead Sea, traditional site of Jesus' baptism.

Machaerus, where John the Baptist was put to death on orders of Herod Antipas.

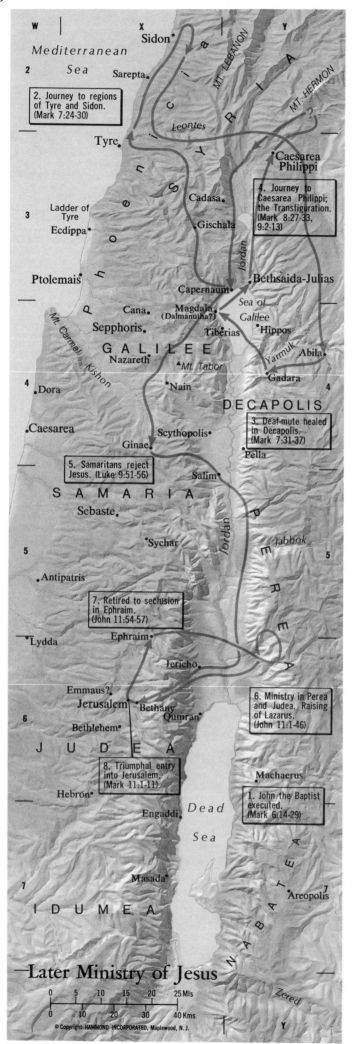

Later Ministry of Jesus

2. Journey to regions of Tyre and Sidon. (Mark 7:24-30)

4. Journey to Caesarea Philippi; the Transfiguration. (Mark 8:27-33, 9:2-13)

3. Deaf-mute healed in Decapolis. (Mark 7:31-37)

5. Samaritans reject Jesus. (Luke 9:51-56)

7. Retired to seclusion in Ephraim. (John 11:54-57)

6. Ministry in Perea and Judea. Raising of Lazarus. (John 11:1-46)

8. Triumphal entry into Jerusalem. (Mark 11:1-11)

1. John the Baptist executed. (Mark 6:14-29)

The Events of Passion Week
(According to the Synoptic Gospels)

	MATT.	MARK	LUKE
SUNDAY (Palm Sunday)			
Triumphal entry into Jerusalem	21:1-9	11:1-10	19:28-44
Visit to Temple and return to Bethany	21:10-17	11:11	19:45-46
MONDAY			
On the way to Jerusalem Jesus curses an unfruitful fig tree	21:18-19	11:12-14	
The Temple court cleansed		11:15-19	19:45-48
TUESDAY			
Returning to Jerusalem, Jesus explains the withering of the fig tree	21:20-22	11:20-26	
Jesus' authority is questioned	21:23-27	11:27-33	20:1-8
Teachings in the Temple	21:28-46; 22	12:1-37a	20:9-44
Condemnation of scribes and Pharisees	23:1-36	12:37b-40	20:45-47
Jesus in Temple treasury calls attention to widow's gift		12:41-44	21:1-4
Prediction of destruction of the Temple and the end of the World	24:1-44	13:1-37	21:5-38
WEDNESDAY			
Conspiracy against Jesus	26:1-5	14:1-2	22:1-2
Anointing at Bethany	26:6-13	14:1-9	
Judas agrees to betray Jesus	26:14-16	14:10-11	22:3-6
THURSDAY (Maundy Thursday)			
Jesus prepares to celebrate Passover	26:17-19	14:12-16	22:7-13
The Last Supper	26:20-29	14:17-25	22:14-38
Withdrawal to Gethsemane	26:30-46	14:26-42	22:39-46
Betrayal and arrest of Jesus	26:47-56	14:43-52	22:47-53
Jesus before Caiaphas and members of the Sanhedrin; Peter's denial	26:57-75	14:53-72	22:54-71
FRIDAY (Good Friday)			
Trial before Pilate; Judas' suicide	27:1-2	15:1-5	23:1-5
Jesus sent to Herod			23:6-16
Pilate imposes sentence of death	27:15-26	15:6-15	23:17-25
Jesus scourged and led to Golgotha	27:27-32	15:15-21	
Jesus' crucifixion and death	27:33-56	15:22-41	23:33-49
Jesus is buried	27:57-61	15:42-47	23:50-56
SATURDAY			
The guarded tomb	27:62-66		
SUNDAY (Easter)			
The empty tomb and the risen Christ	28:1-10	16:1-8	24:1-12

A modern church at ancient Bethany marks the traditional place where Jesus raised Lazarus from the dead (John 11:1-44).

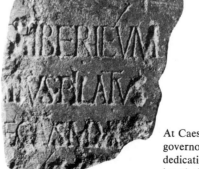

Silver denarius of Tiberius, "tribute money" of Luke 20:21-26.

At Caesarea, residence of the Roman governors, archaeologists found this dedication stone with the only known inscriptional reference to Pontius Pilate.

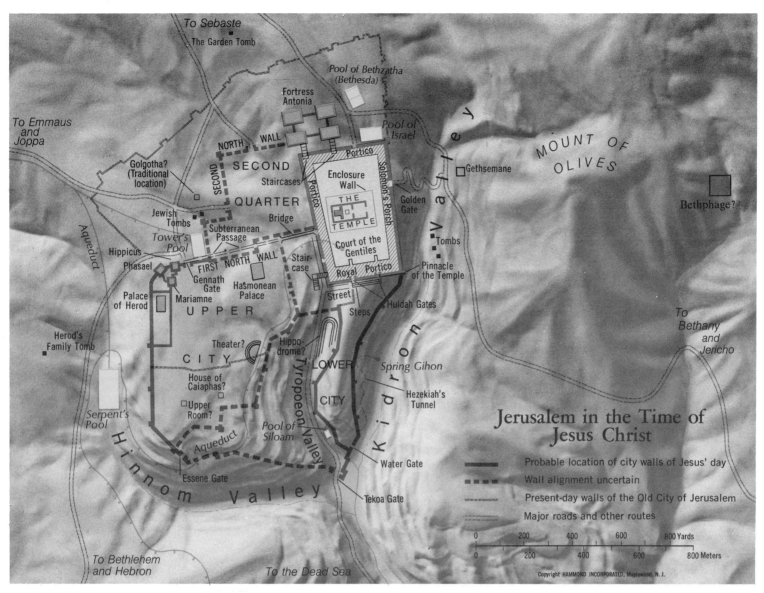

Jerusalem in the Time of Jesus Christ

Probable location of city walls of Jesus' day
Wall alignment uncertain
Present-day walls of the Old City of Jerusalem
Major roads and other routes

0   200   400   600   800 Yards
0   200   400   600   800 Meters

Copyright HAMMOND INCORPORATED, Maplewood, N.J.

Map labels: To Sebaste; The Garden Tomb; Pool of Bethzatha (Bethesda); Fortress Antonia; To Emmaus and Joppa; NORTH WALL; SECOND; Golgotha? (Traditional location); Pool of Israel; MOUNT OF OLIVES; Portico; SECOND QUARTER; Staircases; Enclosure Wall; THE TEMPLE; Solomon's Porch; Gethsemane; Bethphage?; Jewish Tombs; Bridge; Court of the Gentiles; Golden Gate; Aqueduct; Tower's Pool; Subterranean Passage; Hippicus; FIRST NORTH WALL; Staircase; Royal Portico; Pinnacle of the Temple; Tombs; Kidron Valley; Phasael; Gennath Gate; Hasmonean Palace; Street; Palace of Herod; Mariamne; Steps; Huldah Gates; To Bethany and Jericho; UPPER CITY; Herod's Family Tomb; Theater?; Hippo-drome?; Tyropoeon Valley; LOWER CITY; Spring Gihon; House of Caiaphas?; Hezekiah's Tunnel; Serpent's Pool; Upper Room?; Pool of Siloam; Aqueduct; Water Gate; Essene Gate; Hinnom Valley; Tekoa Gate; To Bethlehem and Hebron; To the Dead Sea

Today a mosque, the magnificent Dome of the Rock, occupies the platform where Herod's Temple stood in Jesus' day.

Judas' 30 pieces of silver may have been Tyrian shekels of this type.

A model of Jerusalem shows the Temple platform and four towers of Fortress Antonia. The Pool of Bethzatha where Jesus healed the crippled man is in the foreground.

The Garden Tomb, a rock-cut tomb of the type in which Jesus was buried. North of Jerusalem, this quiet spot just outside the present north wall is a rival to the traditional site of the crucifixion and burial.

"The Pavement" (courtyard) of the Fortress Antonia was possibly the place where Jesus was tried by Pilate. Today it is the crypt of a church and convent.

Theodotus synagogue inscription found on Mount Zion in Jerusalem. Some think this dedicatory inscription refers to the "Synagogue of the Freedmen" mentioned in Acts 6:9.

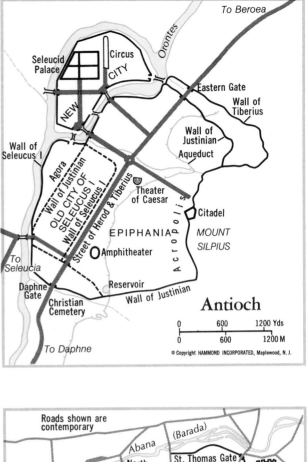

Antioch

The Lion Gate in Jerusalem's east wall. Medieval Christian tradition locates the martyrdom of Stephen (Acts 7:58-60) nearby. Therefore Christians call this "St. Stephen's Gate."

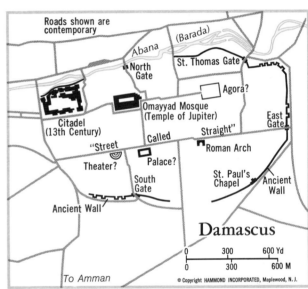

Damascus

St. Paul's Chapel, Damascus. This is the traditional location of Paul's escape over the city wall (Acts 9:25).

The theater by the sea at Caesarea where in 10 B.C. Herod dedicated his splendid new city. Now restored, it is used for concerts.

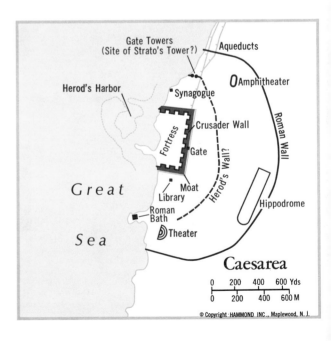

Caesarea

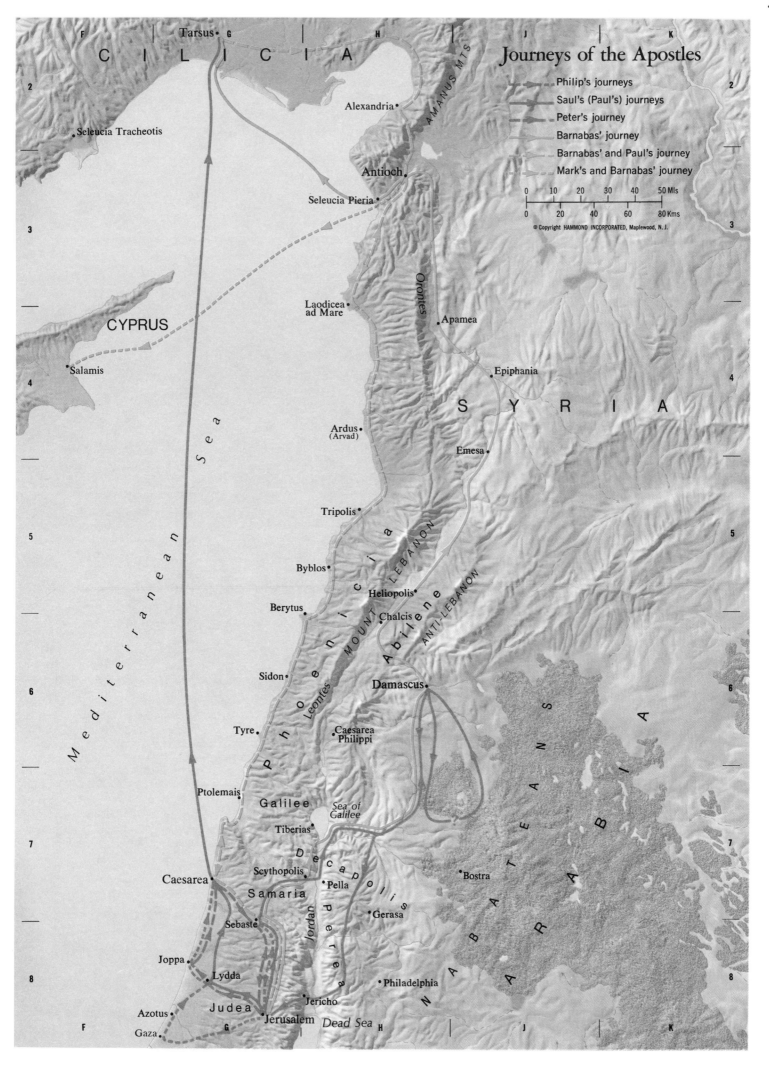

Journeys of the Apostles

- ---- Philip's journeys
- ——— Saul's (Paul's) journeys
- – – – Peter's journey
- ——— Barnabas' journey
- ---- Barnabas' and Paul's journey
- ---- Mark's and Barnabas' journey

| 0 | 10 | 20 | 30 | 40 | 50 Mls |

| 0 | 20 | 40 | 60 | 80 Kms |

© Copyright HAMMOND INCORPORATED, Maplewood, N.J.

CILICIA

Tarsus

Seleucia Tracheotis

Alexandria

Antioch

Seleucia Pieria

AMANUS MTS

Orontes

Apamea

Epiphania

SYRIA

Laodicea ad Mare

CYPRUS

Salamis

Mediterranean Sea

Ardus (Arvad)

Emesa

Tripolis

Byblos

Heliopolis

LEBANON

ANTI-LEBANON

Berytus

Chalcis

Abilene

MOUNT

Phoenicia

Sidon

Damascus

Leontes

Tyre

Caesarea Philippi

Ptolemais

Galilee

Sea of Galilee

Tiberias

Decapolis

NABATEANS

Caesarea

Scythopolis

Pella

Bostra

Samaria

Gerasa

Jordan

Perea

Sebaste

Philadelphia

Joppa

Lydda

Jericho

ARABIA

Azotus

Judea

Jerusalem

Dead Sea

Gaza

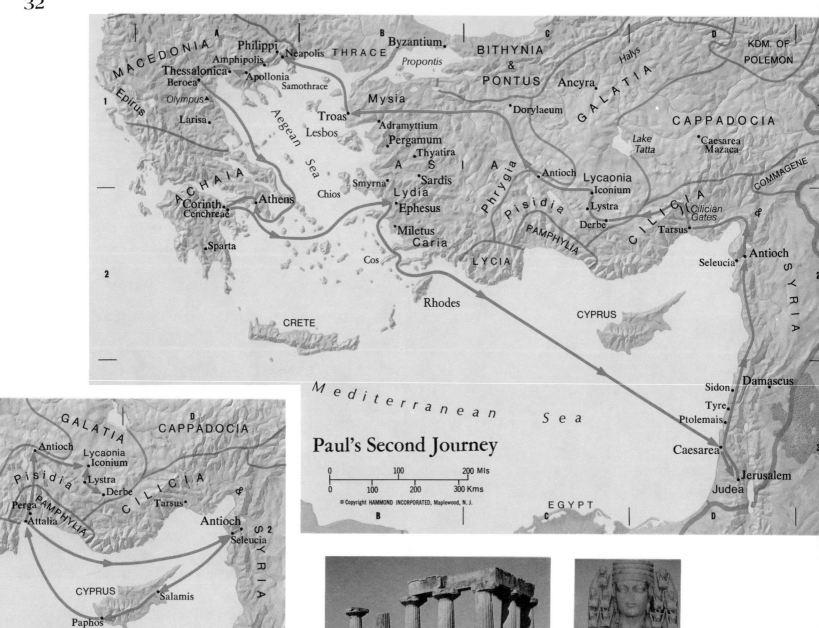

Temple of Apollo, Corinth.
Only 7 of the 38 columns seen
by Paul are now standing.

Artemis was the chief
deity of Ephesus. Paul's
attack on the worship of
this goddess provoked a
riot (Acts 19:23f.).

Paul's Second Journey

0   100   200 Mls
0 100 200 300 Kms
© Copyright HAMMOND INCORPORATED, Maplewood, N. J.

Paul's First Journey

0   100   200 Mls
0 100 200 300 Kms
© Copyright HAMMOND INCORPORATED, Maplewood, N. J.

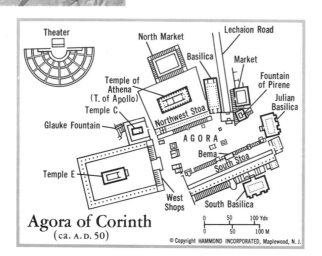

Agora of Corinth
(ca. A.D. 50)

0   50   100 Yds
0   50   100 M
© Copyright HAMMOND INCORPORATED, Maplewood, N. J.

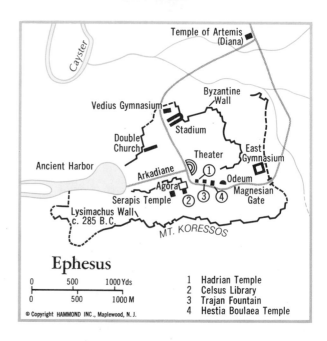

Ephesus

0   500   1000 Yds
0   500   1000 M
© Copyright HAMMOND INC., Maplewood, N. J.

1 Hadrian Temple
2 Celsus Library
3 Trajan Fountain
4 Hestia Boulaea Temple

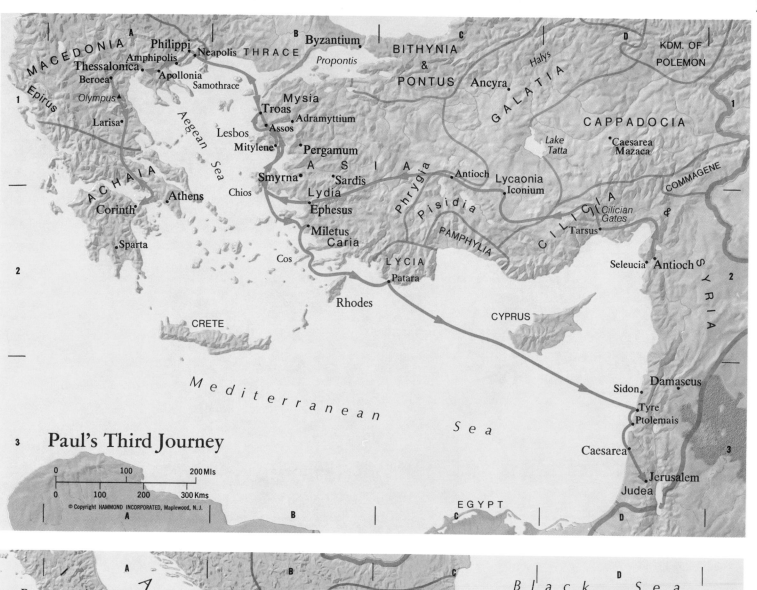

Paul's Third Journey

MACEDONIA
Philippi
Amphipolis
Neapolis
THRACE
Byzantium
BITHYNIA
&
PONTUS
KDM. OF
POLEMON
Thessalonica
Apollonia
Propontis
Ancyra
Halys
GALATIA
Beroea
Samothrace
Epirus
Olympus
Mysia
Troas
Adramyttium
CAPPADOCIA
Larisa
Lesbos
Assos
Lake
Tatta
Caesarea
Mazaca
Aegean
Sea
Mitylene
Pergamum
A S I A
Phrygia
Antioch
COMMAGENE
Smyrna
Sardis
Lycaonia
Iconium
ACHAIA
Chios
Lydia
Pisidia
CILICIA
&
Athens
Ephesus
Tarsus
Cilician
Gates
Corinth
Miletus
Caria
PAMPHYLIA
Sparta
Cos
LYCIA
Seleucia
Antioch
SYRIA
Patara
Rhodes
CYPRUS
CRETE
Damascus
Sidon
Mediterranean
Sea
Tyre
Ptolemais
Caesarea
Judea
Jerusalem
EGYPT

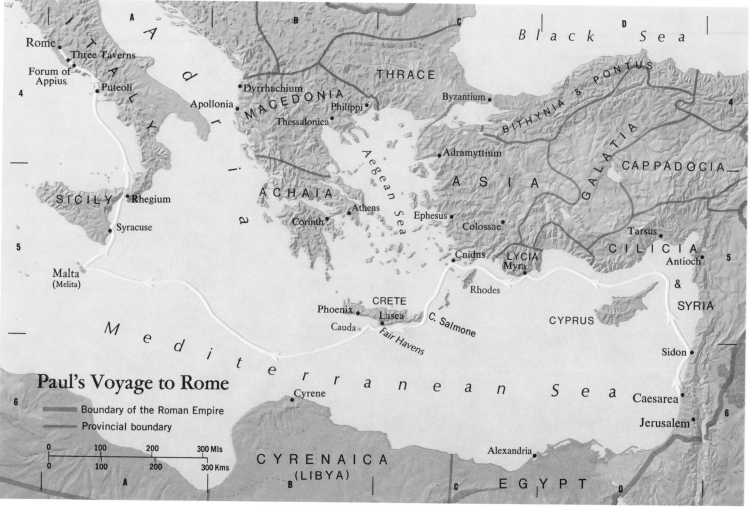

Paul's Voyage to Rome

Rome
Three Taverns
Forum of
Appius
Puteoli
I T A L Y
A d r i a t i c
Black   Sea
Dyrrachium
THRACE
BITHYNIA & PONTUS
Apollonia
MACEDONIA
Philippi
Byzantium
Thessalonica
Adramyttium
CAPPADOCIA
GALATIA
SICILY
Rhegium
ACHAIA
Aegean
Sea
A S I A
Ephesus
Athens
Colossae
Tarsus
Syracuse
Corinth
Cnidus
CILICIA
Malta
(Melita)
LYCIA
Myra
Antioch
&
CRETE
Rhodes
CYPRUS
SYRIA
Phoenix
Lasea
Cauda
Fair Havens
C. Salmone
Sidon
Mediterranean   Sea
Cyrene
Caesarea

Boundary of the Roman Empire
Provincial boundary

Jerusalem
Alexandria
CYRENAICA
(LIBYA)
EGYPT

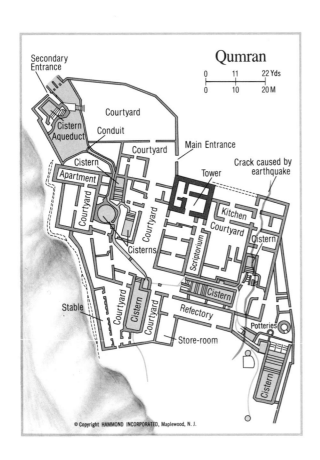

Qumran

Secondary Entrance

Courtyard

Cistern
Aqueduct

Conduit

Courtyard

Main Entrance

Cistern

Crack caused by earthquake

Apartment

Tower

Courtyard

Courtyard

Kitchen

Cistern

Courtyard

Scriptorium

Cisterns

Cistern

Cistern

Stable

Courtyard

Courtyard

Cistern

Refectory

Store-room

Potteries

Cistern

© Copyright HAMMOND INCORPORATED, Maplewood, N.J.

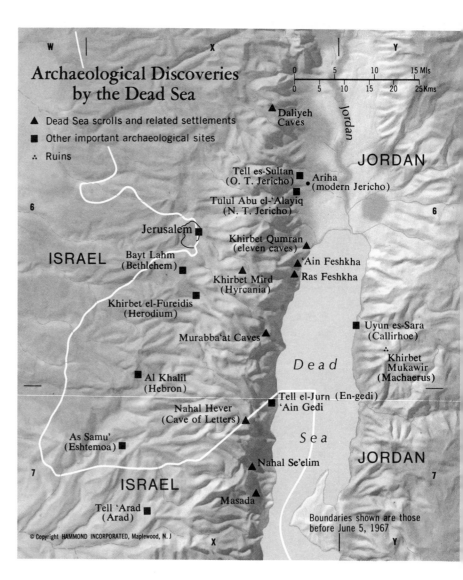

Archaeological Discoveries by the Dead Sea

▲ Dead Sea scrolls and related settlements

■ Other important archaeological sites

∴ Ruins

Daliyeh Caves

JORDAN

Tell es-Sultan (O. T. Jericho) ■   Ariha (modern Jericho)

Tulul Abu el-'Alayiq (N. T. Jericho)

Jerusalem

ISRAEL

Khirbet Qumran (eleven caves) ▲

Bayt Lahm (Bethlehem)

'Ain Feshkha ▲

Khirbet Mird (Hyrcania) ▲

Ras Feshkha ▲

Khirbet el-Fureidis (Herodium)

Murabba'at Caves ▲

Uyun es-Sara (Callirhoe) ■

Dead

Khirbet Mukawir (Machaerus)

Al Khalil (Hebron)

Tell el-Jurn (En-gedi) 'Ain Gedi

Nahal Hever (Cave of Letters) ▲

Sea

As Samu' (Eshtemoa)

JORDAN

Nahal Se'elim ▲

ISRAEL

Masada ▲

Tell 'Arad (Arad)

Boundaries shown are those before June 5, 1967

© Copyright HAMMOND INCORPORATED, Maplewood, N.J

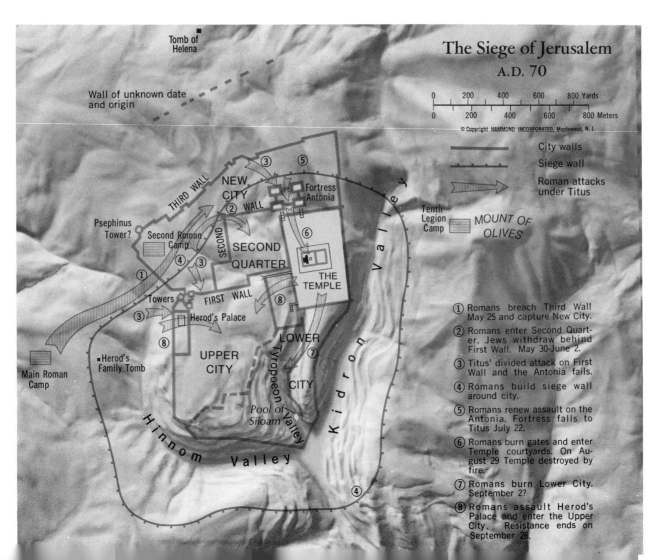

The Siege of Jerusalem
A.D. 70

© Copyright HAMMOND INCORPORATED, Maplewood, N.J.

Tomb of Helena

Wall of unknown date and origin

━━ City walls
━━ Siege wall
⇒ Roman attacks under Titus

THIRD WALL

NEW CITY

WALL

Fortress Antonia

Psephinus Tower?

Second Roman Camp

SECOND

SECOND QUARTER

THE TEMPLE

Tenth Legion Camp

MOUNT OF OLIVES

Kidron Valley

Towers

FIRST WALL

Herod's Palace

LOWER CITY

Main Roman Camp

Herod's Family Tomb

UPPER CITY

Tyropoeon Valley

Pool of Siloam

Hinnom Valley

① Romans breach Third Wall May 25 and capture New City.

② Romans enter Second Quarter. Jews withdraw behind First Wall. May 30–June 2.

③ Titus' divided attack on First Wall and the Antonia fails.

④ Romans build siege wall around city.

⑤ Romans renew assault on the Antonia. Fortress falls to Titus July 22.

⑥ Romans burn gates and enter Temple courtyards. On August 29 Temple destroyed by fire.

⑦ Romans burn Lower City. September 2?

⑧ Romans assault Herod's Palace and enter the Upper City. Resistance ends on September 26.

Cave Four (center) at Qumran, in which a wealth of precious scrolls were found.

Masada, the impregnable rock fortress of Herod the Great, was the last stronghold of the Jews in the revolt against Rome.

Masada

The First Jewish Revolt

- •••••• Border of areas in revolt A.D. 66
- Area lost by Jews in 67
- Area lost by Jews in 68
- Remaining Jewish strongholds given up to Romans 70-73
- Roman siege
- Jewish fort
- 11 Dates of Roman campaigns
- → Under Gallus 66
- → Under Vespasian 66-68
- → Under Titus 70
- → Under Bassus 71
- → Under Silva 73

© Copyright HAMMOND INCORPORATED, Maplewood, N.J.

The Great Sea (Mediterranean Sea)

Silver shekel from "the year two," the second year of the Revolt, A.D. 67.

Roman "Judaea Capta" coins. Above are Vespasian and Titus. Sestertius, right, shows a captive Jewess.

The Spread of Christianity

The Seven Churches of Asia (Rev. 1-3)

City with Christian church recorded in second century

Regions known to contain Christians by A.D. 185 (the time of Irenaeus)

Boundary of the Roman empire for most of second century

Temporarily controlled by Rome

0 100 200 300 400 500Mls
0 200 400 600 800Kms

© Copyright HAMMOND INCORPORATED, Maplewood, N.J.

St. Paul's-Outside-the-Walls, Rome, traditional site of the tomb of Paul.

The Flavian Amphitheater (Colosseum) in Rome, where many Christians were martyred.

Constantine made Christianity a "legal religion" in A.D. 311.

The Seven Churches of Asia Minor

Chalice of Antioch shows Christ and apostles. It dates from 4th or 5th century A.D.

Patmos, where The Revelation to St. John the Divine, the last book in the New Testament, was written.

Papyrus fragment of the Gospel of Matthew from Qxyrhynchus, Egypt.

The four-spouted oil lamp (top)
is from Patriarchal times;
the Herodian lamp (bottom)
is typical of Jesus' day.

The Moabite Stone, found in 1868
at Mesha's capital. Carved about
840-820 B.C., it tells of the events of
2 Kings 3:4-27 and their aftermath
from a Moabite point of view.

The mound of Tell el-Hesi. One of
the first sites to be excavated in
Palestine, it is thought to be
Biblical Eglon, a Canaanite royal
city taken by Joshua (Joshua 10).

Archaeological Sites
in Israel and Jordan

■ Principal excavated sites
T, Tel, Tell: city site or mound
Kh, Khirbet: ruin

© Copyright by HAMMOND INC., Maplewood, N.J.

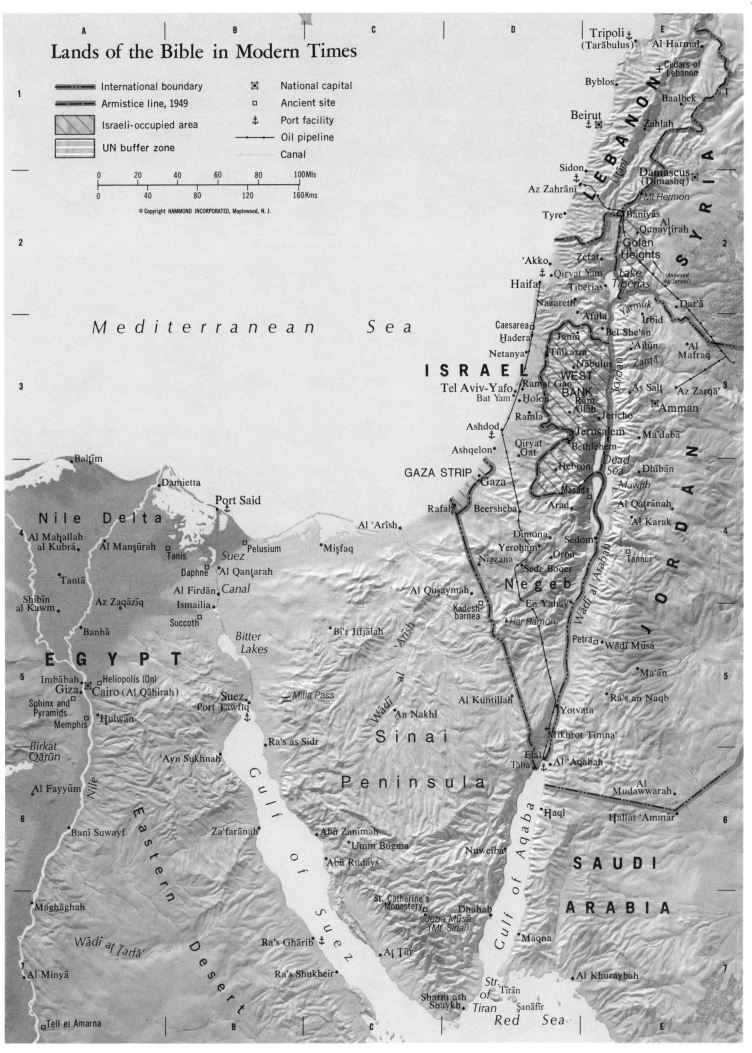

Lands of the Bible in Modern Times

‗‗‗‗ International boundary	⊚	National capital
‗‗‗‗ Armistice line, 1949	▫	Ancient site
⧄ Israeli-occupied area	⚓	Port facility
▤ UN buffer zone	•—•—	Oil pipeline
	⋯⋯	Canal

```
0    20    40    60    80    100 Mls
0     40    80    120    160 Kms
```

© Copyright HAMMOND INCORPORATED, Maplewood, N.J.

M e d i t e r r a n e a n   S e a

Tripoli⚓
(Tarābulus) • Al Harmal
Cedars of Lebanon
Byblos • Baalbek
Beirut⚓⊚ Zahlah
Sidon⚓ Damascus (Dimashq)⊚
Az Zahrānī •Mt.Hermon
Tyre •Bāniyās
Al Qunayṭirah
Golan Heights (Annexed by Israel)
'Akko Zefat
Qiryat Yam Lake Tiberias
Haifa Tiberias
Nazareth Yarmuk Dar'ā
Afula Irbid
Caesarea Jenin Bet She'an 'Ajlūn Al Mafraq
Hadera Ṭūlkarm Zarqā'
Netanya Nābulus As Salṭ Az Zarqā'
ISRAEL WEST BANK
Tel Aviv-Yafo Ramat Gan Rām Allāh Amman
Bat Yam Holon Jericho
Ramla Ma'daba
Ashdod⚓ Jerusalem
Qiryat Gat Bethlehem Dead Sea Dhībān
Ashqelon Hebron Mawjib
GAZA STRIP Masada Al Qaṭrānah
Gaza Arad Al Karak
Rafah Beersheba
Al 'Arīsh Dimona Sedom Tannūr
Mişfaq Yeroham Oron
Nizzana Sede Boqer
Negeb Petra Wādī Mūsá
Bi'r Jifjālah Kadesh-barnea Ma'ān
Har Ramon Ra's an Naqb
Al Quṣaymah
An Nakhl Al Kuntillah Yotvata
Elat Al 'Aqabah
Ṭaba⚓
Al Mudawwarah
Ḥaql Ḥallat 'Ammār
SAUDI ARABIA

Nile Delta
Balṭūm
Damietta
Port Said⚓
Al Maḥallah al Kubrá
Al Manṣūrah
Tanis *Suez* Pelusium
Daphne Al Qanṭarah
Tanṭā Al Firdān *Canal*
Az Zaqāzīq Ismailia
Shibīn al Kawm Succoth
Banhā
E G Y P T
Bitter Lakes
Imbābah Heliopolis (On)
Giza Cairo (Al Qāhirah)
Sphinx and Pyramids Ḥulwān
Memphis
Birkat Qārūn
Al Fayyūm
Suez⚓ Mitla Pass
Port Tawfīq
Ra's as Sidr
'Ayn Sukhnah
Wādī al *'Arīsh*
Wādī al *Arabah*
S i n a i
P e n i n s u l a
Eastern Desert
Gulf of Suez
Gulf of Aqaba
Māghāghah
Za'farānah Abū Zanimah
Umm Bugma
Abū Rudays
Nuweiba
Wādī aṭ Ṭarfā'
Ra's Ghārib⚓ Maqna
Aṭ Ṭūr
Al Minyā Ra's Shukheir
St. Catherine's Monastery
Jaba Mūsá (Mt. Sinai)
Dhahab
Tell el Amarna
Sharm ash Shaykh
Ṣanāfīr
Str. of Tiran Tirān
Al Khuraybah
Red Sea

LEBANON **SYRIA** **JORDAN** Litani Jordan

Time Chart of Bible History

DATE	PALESTINE	EGYPT	MESOPOTAMIA & PERSIA	ANATOLIA & SYRIA	GREECE & ROME
4000 BC	Neolithic culture (Jericho) Ghassulian culture c.3500 The Canaanites, a Semitic people, were ancestral to the Phoenicians Early Bronze urban culture c.3300 Amorite invasions c.2500-2300	— First use of metal: copper and bronze — Hieroglyphic writing developed **Archaic Period** Menes unifies Egypt **Old Kingdom** The Great Pyramids at Gizeh c.2550 Old Kingdom falls	Halaf culture Cuneiform writing developed Sumerian city states c.2800-2360 **Akkadian Empire** Sargon I 2360-2305 Gutian kings Ur dominance	Early Bronze cities Byblos, Troy, Ugarit Syria under Akkadian Empire Hittites enter Anatolia	Beginning of Minoan civilization on Crete Greeks invade Balkan peninsula
2000 BC	Egypt controls Canaan Abraham — oral tradition Israelite sojourn in Egypt Battle of Megiddo 1468 Amarna letters c.1370-1353 The Exodus c.1290 Israelite invasion Philistine penetration Kdm. of Saul c.1020-1000	**Middle Kingdom** Hyksos invaders from Asia c.1720-1550 **New Kingdom** Akhenaton 1370-1353 Tutankhamen 1353-1344 Ramses II 1290-1224 Ramses III defeats Sea Peoples c.1170 **Late Dynastic Period**	Ur falls c.1950 **Isin-Larsa Period** **Old Babylonian Empire** Hammurabi 1728-1686 **Kassite Period** Hittites sack Babylon 1531 Mitanni Kdm. **Rise of Assyria** Shalmaneser I Tiglath-pileser I 1115-1078	Amorite invasions Hittites intro. Iron Labarnas I c.1600 **Old Hittite Kingdom** Mursilis I c.1540 Suppilullumas **Hittite Empire** Battle of Kedesh 1296 Sack of Troy 1192	**Minoan Sea Empire** Mycenae shaft graves Cretan palaces destroyed c.1400 Dorians invade Greece Trojan War c.1200
1000 BC	**United Kingdom** David c.1000-961 Solomon c.961-922 First Temple completed c.950 **Divided Kingdom** Rehoboam & Jeroboam I Omri dynasty 876-842 Samaria founded c.875 Jehu dynasty 842-745	Period of decline Shishak c.935-914 Libyan dynasties 950-710	**Assyrian Empire** Asshurnasirpal II 883-859 Shalmaneser III 859-824 Adad-nirari III 807-782	Arameans flood into Syria Hiram of Tyre 969-936 Damascus city state Ben-hadad II Battle of Qarqar 853 Phoenicians found Carthage 814	Decline of Aegean Bronze Age civilization Latins settle in central Italy
800 BC 600 BC	Israel resurgence under Jeroboam II 786-746 Amos, Hosea Fall of Samaria and exile of Israel 722/721 Hezekiah of Judah 715-687/6 Isaiah Micah Judah resurgence under Josiah 640-609 Jeremiah	Nubian dynasties 715-663 Egypt under Assyrian rule 671-652 Thebes sacked 663 Neco II 609-593	Tiglath-pileser III 745-727 Sargon II 722-705 Sennacherib 705-681 Asshurbanapal 669-633 Rise of Babylon under Nabopolassar Fall of Nineveh to Medes and Babylonians 612	Phrygian Kdm. Midas c.715 Lydian Kdm. Gyges of Lydia 680-652	First Olympics 776 Legendary founding of Rome 753 Etruscan period Homer Draco codifies Athenian law 621

Kings of Judah and Israel

JUDAH	ISRAEL	JUDAH	ISRAEL
Rehoboam 922-915	922-901 Jeroboam I	Jotham 750-735	746-745 Zechariah
Abijah 915-913	901-900 Nadab		745 Shallum
Asa 913-873	900-877 Baasha		745-738 Menahem
	877-876 Elah		738-737 Pekahiah
	876 Zimri	Ahaz 735-715	737-732 Pekah
Jehoshaphat 873-849	876-869 Omri		732-724 Hoshea
	869-850 Ahab	Hezekiah 715-687/6	722/721 Fall of Samaria
	850-849 Ahaziah	Manasseh 687/6-642	
Jehoram 849-842	849-842 Jehoram	Amon 642-640	
Ahaziah 842	842-815 Jehu	Josiah 640-609	
Athaliah 842-837		Jehoahaz 609	
Joash 837-800	815-801 Jehoahaz	Jehoiakim 609-598	
Amaziah 800-783	801-786 Jehoash	Jehoiachin 598-597	
Uzziah 783-742	786-746 Jeroboam II	Zedekiah 597-587	

Fall of Jerusalem 587

DATE	PALESTINE	EGYPT	MESOPOTAMIA & PERSIA	ANATOLIA & SYRIA	GREECE & ROME
600 BC	Destruction of Jerusalem and exile of Judah 587 Ezekiel **Babylonian Captivity** Edict of Cyrus allows return of Jews 538 Zerubbabel Temple rebuilt 520-515 **Persian Period** Ezra's mission 458?? Nehemiah comes to Judah 445 (440?)	Egypt under Persian rule 525-401 Unsuccessful revolt Return to native rule	**New Babylonian Empire** Nebuchadnezzar II 605-562 **Persian Empire** Cyrus 550-530 Babylon falls 539 Cambyses 530-522 Darius I 522-486 Xerxes I 486-465 Artaxerxes I Darius II 433-404	Syria and Anatolia under Persian rule Phoenicians provide fleet for Persian attacks on Greece	Solon's judicial reforms c.590 Rome ruled by Etruscan kings Roman Republic established 509 Persian Wars 499-479 Thermopylae-Salamis 480 Pericles 461-429 Herodotus
400 BC	Ezra's mission 398? Palestine passes under Alexander's rule and Hellenization begins 332 Ptolemaic Egyptian rule 312	Persian rule 342-332 Alexander conquers Egypt 332 Ptolemy I 323-284 **Ptolemaic Kingdom** Alexandrian Jews translate Pentateuch into Greek Ptolemy V 203-181	Artaxerxes III 358-338 Alexander invades Persia 331 Seleucid rule Parthians and Bactrians gain independence c.250	Alexander takes Tyre 332 Seleucid rule Seleucus I 312-280 **Seleucid Empire** Antiochus I 280-261 Seleucus II 246-226 Antiochus III (The Great) 223-187	Socrates' death Sack of Rome by Gauls Philip II of Macedon Alexander the Great 336-323 **Alexander's Empire** Wars of the Diodochi 1st and 2nd Punic Wars Hannibal in Italy 218
200 BC	Palestine comes under Seleucid Syrian control 198 **Maccabean Period** Judas Maccabeus leads revolt of Jews 166-160 Temple rededicated 164 Jonathan 160-142 Simon 142-134 John Hyrcanus I 134-104 Aristobulus I 104-103	Ptolemy VI 181-146 Antiochus IV campaigns in Egypt Ptolemy VII 146-116	**Parthian Empire** Mithridates I 171-138 Mithridates II 124-88	Battle of Magnesia 190 Antiochus IV (Epiphanes) 175-163 Antiochus V 163-162 Demetrius I 162-150 Demetrius II 145-139 Tyre independent	Spain annexed by Rome **Empire of the Roman Republic** 3rd Punic War Romans destroy Carthage and Corinth 146 Reforms of the Gracchi
100 BC **50 BC**	Alexander Jannaeus 103-76 Alexandra 76-67 Aristobulus II 67-63 Pompey takes Jerusalem for Rome 63 Hyrcanus II, high priest 63-40 Antipater governor 55	Ptolemy VIII 116-81 Ptolemy XI 80-81 Cleopatra VII 51-30	Tigranes of Armenia Phrates III 70-57 Orodes I 57-38 War with Rome 55-38 Crassus defeated	Mithridatic Wars Antiochus XIII 68-67 Anatolia and Syria under Roman control	Sulla dictator 82-79 1st Triumvirate Pompey's campaigns in Asia 66-63 Caesar's Gallic Wars 58-51

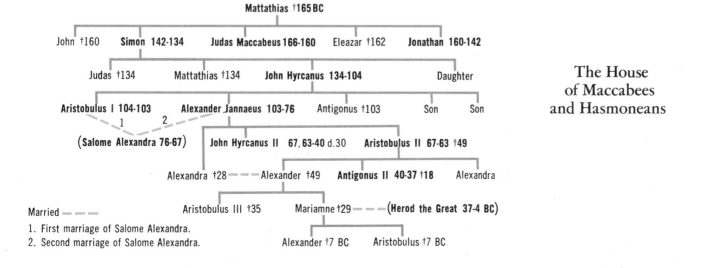

The House of Maccabees and Hasmoneans

Married - - -
1. First marriage of Salome Alexandra.
2. Second marriage of Salome Alexandra.

Time Chart of Bible History, Continued

DATE	PALESTINE	THE WEST	THE EAST
50 BC	**Roman Rule** Caesar in Judea 47 Parthian invasion 40 Antigonus 40-37 Herod the Great 37-4 BC Herod's Temple begun 18 Birth of Christ c. 4 BC Archelaus 4 BC-AD 6	Death of Pompey 48 Death of Caesar 44 2nd Triumvirate Battle of Philippi 42 Battle of Actium 31 Augustus — First emperor 27 BC-AD 14 **Roman Empire**	**Parthian Empire** Phraates 37-32 Parthians defeat Antony 36
0	Roman governors 6-41 Pontius Pilate 27-37 Death of Christ c. 29 Herod Agrippa I 41-44 Paul's 1st journey, Council at Jerusalem 46/47	Varus defeated in Germany 9 Tiberius 14-37 Gaius (Caligula) 37-41 Claudius 41-54 Conquest of Britain begun 43	Artabanus II 10-40
50 AD	Antonius Felix 52-60 Imprisonment of Paul 58 Porcius Festus 60-62 Paul sent to Rome 60 Gessius Florus 64-66 First Jewish Revolt 66-73 Destruction of Jerusalem 70 Fall of Masada 73 Jewish center at Jamnia	Nero 54-68 1st Persecution of Christians 64 Galba, Otho, Vitellius 68/69 Vespasian 69-79 Titus 79-81 Domitian 81-96 Nerva 96-98 Trajan 98-117	Vologases I 51-80 Parthian War with Rome 53-63 Osroes (Chosroes) 89-128
100 AD **135 AD**	Jewish uprisings in Palestine, Egypt, Mesopotamia 116-117 Bar-Kochba Revolt 132-135 Jerusalem razed, Aelia Capitolina built on site	Campaigns in Dacia 101-107 Hadrian 117-138	Conquest of Nabateans by Romans Trajan invades Parthia 114 Territory lost to Romans regained 118

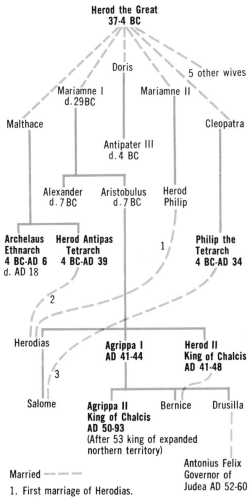

Herod and His Descendants

Herod the Great
37-4 BC

Doris — 5 other wives

Mariamne I d. 29 BC — Mariamne II

Malthace — Cleopatra

Antipater III d. 4 BC

Alexander d. 7 BC — Aristobulus d. 7 BC — Herod Philip

Archelaus Ethnarch 4 BC-AD 6 d. AD 18 — **Herod Antipas Tetrarch 4 BC-AD 39** — 1 — **Philip the Tetrarch 4 BC-AD 34**

2

Herodias — **Agrippa I AD 41-44** — **Herod II King of Chalcis AD 41-48**

3

Salome — **Agrippa II King of Chalcis AD 50-93** (After 53 king of expanded northern territory) — Bernice — Drusilla

Antonius Felix Governor of Judea AD 52-60

Married - - - -

1. First marriage of Herodias.
2. Second marriage of Herodias.
3. Salome, daughter of Herodias and Herod (sometimes referred to as Philip), danced before Herod Antipas for John the Baptist's head. She married her great-uncle Philip the Tetrarch.

d. died

Roman catapult. A type of artillery used effectively by both Romans and Jews in the battle for Jerusalem, A.D. 69-70.

Gazetteer-Index

This Gazetteer-Index is an alphabetical listing of all geographical names found on the maps of this volume. The spelling of Biblical names used on maps and index is that found in the Revised Standard Version (RSV). Alternative Biblical or other ancient names are given in parentheses. Wherever possible, the modern equivalent (Arabic, Hebrew, Turkish, etc.) of an ancient name is given in italic type. A question mark after the identification of a site indicates that the location is possible or probable but not yet certain. The page numbers of the maps on which the name appears are listed in sequence. The key or grid reference (a letter-figure combination) following the page number(s) refers to the letters and figures at the margins of the maps. For example, Azotus (Ashdod in Old Testament times) [Arabic *Isdud*, Hebrew *Tel Ashdod*] can be found on the maps on pages 23, 25, 26 and 35 at key reference W6 and on page 31 at G8. Entries for locations within or near Jerusalem give the page numbers only for the appropriate Jerusalem maps.

ABBREVIATIONS

T. = Tell, Tel (mound)
Kh. = Khirbet (ruin)
H. = Horvat (ruin)
J. = Jebel (hill or mount)
W. = Wadi (seasonal stream)

A

Abana, *Nahr Barada*, river. 4:Z2
Able, (Abel-beth-maachah), *T. Abil.* 12, 14, 15:Y3; 13:H5
Abel-meholah, *T. Abu Sus.* 15:X5
Abila, *T. Abil,* in Decapolis. 23, 25, 26, 27, 28, 38:Y4
Abila, *T. Abila,* in Abilene. 25, 26:Z2
Abilene, region. 25, 26:X2; 31:H6
Abū Rudays. 39:C6
Abū Zanimah. 39:C6
Abydos, *Arabet el-Madfuneh,* in Egypt. 9, 16:F6
Abydos, *Canakkale,* in Asia Minor. 16:E2
Accaron, *see* Ekron
Acco, (Ptolemais, Acre), *'Akko, T. el-Fukhkhar.* 4, 11, 12, 14, 15, 19, 23, 38:X3; 8:B4; 10:D2; 13:G5
Accrabbah, (Akrabatta), *'Aqraba.* 19:X5
Achaean League. 21, 22:C1
Achaia, Roman province. 32, 33:A1; 36:F3
Achmetha, *see* Ecbatana
Achzib, (Ecdippa), *es-Zib.* 11, 12, 19, 38:X3
Achzib-Acco, region. 19:X3
Acra, in Jerusalem. 22
Adasa, *Kh. 'Addasa.* 23:X6
Adida, (Hadid), *el-Haditheh.* 23, 35:W5
Adora, (Adoraim), *Dura.* 23, 25:W6
Adoraim, (Adora), *Dura.* 12, 15:W6
Adramyttium, *Edremit.* 32, 33:B1; 33:C4
Adria, (Adriatic Sea). 33:A4
Adullam, *T. esh-Sheikh Madhkur.* 11, 12, 15, 19, 23:X6
Aegean Sea. 17, 20, 32, 33:A1
Aenon, spring north of *Kh. Umm el-'Umdan* (?). 26:X5
Aetolian League. 21, 22:C1
Africa, Roman province. 36:C4
'Afula. 39:D3
Agade, *Abu Ghubar* (?). 9:J4
Agrippias, (Anthedon), *el-Blahiyeh.* 25,26:V6
Agrippina, *Kaukab el-Hawa.* 26, 27:X4
Ahlab, *Kh. el-Mahalib.* 11:X2
Ai, *et-Tell.* 8:B6; 10:E3; 11, 12, 19, 38:X6
Aijalou, *Yalo.* 11, 12, 15:X6
Aijalon, Valley of, *W. Selman.* 4, 11, 12:W6
'Ain el-Qudeirat, (Kadesh-barnea). 38:V8
'Ain Feshkha, spring. 34, 38:X6
'Ain Gedi, (En-gedi). 34, 38:X7
'Ain Ghazzal. 38:Y5

'Ain Karim. 38:X6
'Ajlūn. 39:E3
Akhetaton, *Tell el-Amarna.* 8:E5; 10:A7
Akkad, region. 9:J4
'Akko, (Acco, Ptolemais). 39:D2
Akrabatta, (Accrabbah), *'Aqraba.* 35:X5
Akrabattene, region. 23:X8
Akrabbim, Ascent of, *Naqb es-Safa.* 15:X8
Alaca Huyuk. 9:G1
Alalakh. 9:G3
Al 'Aqabah. 39:D5
Al 'Arīsh. 39:C4
Alashiya, (Cyprus). 9:F3
Aleppo, (Haleb), *Halab.* 16:G3
Alexandria, *Alexandretta,* in Syria. 31:H2
Alexandria, *Gulashkird,* in Carmania. 20:E4
Alexandria, *Iskandariyeh,* in Egypt. 20:B3; 21, 22:D2; 33:66; 37:G5; *see also city plan p. 21*
Alexandria Arachosiorum, *Ghazni.* 20:F3
Alexandria Arion, *Herat.* 20:F3
Alexandria Eschata, *Khodzent.* 21:G2
Alexandrium, *Qarn Sartabeh.* 23, 25, 26:X5
Al Fayyūm. 39:A6
Al Firdān. 39:B4
Al Harmal. 39:E1
Al Karak. 39:E4
Al Khalil, (Hebron). 34:X6
Al Khuraybah. 39:D7
Al Kuntillah. 39:D5
Al Mafraq. 39:E3
Al Mahallah al Kubra. 39:A4
Al Manşurah. 39:A4
Al Minyā. 39:A7
Al Mudawwarah. 39:E6
Al Qāhirah, (Cairo). 39:A5
Al Qantarah. 39:B4
Al Qatrānah. 39:E4
Al Qunayţirah. 39:E2
Al Qusaymah. 39:D4
Alush, *Wadi el-Esh* (?). 10:C6
Amalek, Amalekites, people. 12:X6; 13:G7; 14:W8
Amanus Mts. 31:H2
Amarna, Tell el-, (Akhetaton). 10, 39:A7
Amastris. 37:G3
Amathus, *T. 'Ammata.* 23, 25, 26:Y5
Amisus. 37:H3
Amman, (Rabba, Philadelphia). 38:Y5; 39:E3
Ammon, region. 4, 11, 12, 14, 15, 19:Z5; 8:C5; 10:E3; 13:H6; 16:G4
Amon, Temple of, *Siwa.* 18, 20:A3
Amorites, people. 8:B6

Amphipolis, *Neochori.* 32, 33:A1
Anab, *Kh. 'Anab es-Saghireh.* 12:W6
Anat, *'Anah.* 16:H4; 17:C3
Anathoth, *Res el-Kharrubeh.* 12, 19:X6
Anchialus. 37:G3
Ancyra, *Ankara.* 16:F2; 18, 20:B2; 32, 33:C1; 37:G3
Ankuwa, *Alisar Huyuk.* 9:G2
An Nakhl. 39:C5
Anthedon, (Agrippias), *el-Blahiyeh.* 23, 25:V6
Anti-Lebanon, mts. 4:Y2; 8:C2; 31:J5
Antioch, *Antakya,* in Syria. 22:D1; 31:H3; 32, 33:D2; 37:H4; *see also city plan p. 30*
Antioch, *Yalvac,* in Pisidia. 32:C1; 32:C2; 37:G3
Antipatris, (Aphek), *Ras el-'Ain.* 25, 26, 28, 35, 38:W5
Antium, *Anzio.* 36:D3
Antonia Fortress, in Jerusalem. 25, 29, 34
Apamea, *Qal'at el-Mudiq.* 31, 37:H4
Aphairema, (Ephraim, Ophrah), *et-Taiyibeh* (?). 23:X5
Aphek, (Antipatris), *Ras el- 'Ain.* 10:D3; 11, 12, 14, 15, 38:X5
Aphek, *Fiq,* in Transjordan. 15:Y4
Aphek, *T. Kurdaneh,* in Asher. 11, 12:X3
Apollonia, *Arsuf,* in Palestine. 19, 23, 25, 26, 35:W5
Apollonia, *Pollinia,* in Macedonia. 32, 33:A1
Apollonia, *Sozopol,* on Black Sea. 18:B1
Appius, Forum of, (Appi Forum). 33:A4
Aqaba, Gulf of. 10, 39:D6
Ar, *el-Misna'.* 14, 15:Y7
Arabah, *el-Ghor, Wadi al 'Arabah.* 4, 15:X8; 10:D5; 13:H8; 39:E4
Arabia, region. 9:H5; 18, 20:C3; 21, 22:E2; 37:J5
Arabian Sea. 21:F4
Arabs, people. 16:H5; 17:C3
Arachosia, region. 18, 20:F3
Arad, (Great Arad), *T. 'Arad.* 8:B7; 10:D4; 11, 12, 14, 15, 23, 34, 38:X7; 13:G6; 39:D3
Arad of Beth-yeroham, *T. el-Milh.* 15, 38:X7
Aral Sea. 17, 18, 20:E1
Aram, (Syria), region. 14, 15:Y2
Aram-Damascus, region. 13:H4
Arameans, people. 11:Y2
Aram-zobah, region. 13:J4
Araq, el-Emir, (Tyrus). 38:Y6
Ararat, (Urartu), region. 16:H2
Ararat, Mt., *Buyuk Agri Dagi.* 9, 16:J2

Araxes, river. 9:K2; 16:J2; 18:D1
Arbela, *Erbil,* in Assyria. 9, 16:J3; 18, 20:D2
Arbela, *Irbid,* in Decapolis. 26:Y4
Arbela, *Kh. Irbid,* in Galilee. 23:X4
Archelais, *Kh. 'Auja et-Tahta.* 26:X5
Ardus, (Arvad), *Erwad, Ruwad.* 31:H4
Areopolis, (Rabbath-moab), *Kh. er-Rabba.* 26, 28:Y7
Argob, region. 13:H5; 14:Y3
Aria, region. 18, 21:F3
Aribi, (Arabs), people. 16:H4
Ariha, (Jericho). 34:X6
Arimathea, (Ramathaim), *Rentis.* 26:X5
'Arish, Wadi al-, (River of Egypt). 4:V8; 39:C5
Armenia, region. 18, 20:C2; 21, 22:E1; 37:J3
Arnon, *W. al-Mawjib,* river. 4, 11, 12, 14, 15, 19, 23, 25, 26, 35:Y7; 8:B6; 10:E4
Aroer, *'Ara'ir,* in Moab. 11, 12, 38:Y6; 13:H6
Arpad, *T. Erfad.* 16:G3
Arvad, (Ardus), *Erwad, Ruwad.* 9, 16:G3; 13:H3; 18:C3; 31:H4
Arzawa, region. 8:E2
Ascalon, (Ashkelon), *'Ashqelon.* 23, 25, 26, 35, 38:W6
Ashdod, (Azotus), *Isdud, T. Ashdod.* 8:A6; 11, 12, 14, 15, 19, 23, 38:W6; 10, 39:D3
Ashdod, region. 19:W6
Ashdod Yam. 38:W6
Asher, tribe. 11, 12:X3
Ashkelon, (Ascalon), *'Ashqelon.* 8:A6; 10:D3; 11, 12, 14, 15, 19, 23, 38:W6; 13:G6
'Ashqelon. 39:D3
Ashtaroth, *T. 'Ashtarah.* 8:C4; 10:E2; 11, 12, 14, 15:Y4; 13:H5
Asia, Roman province. 32, 33:B1; 33:C5; 37:G3
Asia Minor, region. 20:B2
Asochis, *Kh. el-Lon.* 26, 27:X4
Asphaltitis, Lake, (Dead Sea). 25, 26, 35:X6
As Salţ. 39:E3
As Samu', (Eshtemoa). 34:X7
Asshur, *Qal'at Sherqat.* 9:J3; 16:J3; 18:C2
Assos, *Behramkoy.* 33:B1
Assuwa, region. 8:E1
Assyria, region. 9:J3; 16:H3; 17:C2
Assyriau Empire. 16:G4
Astacus. 16:F2
Astorga. 36:A2
Ataroth, *Kh. Attarus.* 15:Y6
Athens. 17, 18, 20, 32, 33:A2; 21, 22:C1; 36:F4
'Atlit, (Pilgrims Castle). 38:W4
Attalia, *Antalya.* 32:C2

Pella, in Macedonia.
20:A2; 21, 22:C1
Pella, *Kh. Fahil.* 19, 23, 25, 26, 28, 35, 38:Y4; 31:H7; 37:H4
Pelusium, (Sin), *T. Farama.* 10, 39:B4; 16:F5; 18, 20:B3
Penuel, *Tulul edh-Dhahab.* 8:B5; 15:Y5
Perea, region. 25, 26, 28, 35:Y5; 31:H8
Perga, *Murtana.* 32:C2; 37:G4
Pergamum, *Bergama.* 21, 22:C1; 32, 33:B1; 37:G3
Persepolis, (Parsa), *Takht-i-Jamshid.* 18, 20:E3
Persia, Persis, region. 17, 18, 20:E3
Persian Empire. 18, 19
Persian Gulf, (Lower Sea). 9:L5; 17, 20:D4; 21, 22:E2
Petra. 39:E5
Pharathon, (Pirathon), *Far'ata.* 23:X5
Pharpar, *Nahr el-'Awaj,* river. 4:Z2
Phasaelis, *Kh. Fasa'il.* 25, 26:X5
Phasael Tower, in Jerusalem. 29
Phaselis, in Lycia. 16:F3
Phasis, *Poti.* 18:C1
Phenice, *see* Phoenix.
Philadelphia, *Alashehir,* in Asia Minor. 37:G3
Philadelphia, (Rabbah), *Amman.* 23, 25, 26, 35:Y5; 31:H8
Philippi, (Colonia Augusta Julia Philippensis), *Filibedjik.* 32, 33:A1; 36:F3
Philistia, region. 12, 14, 15, 23:W6; 13:G6
Philistia, Plain of. 4:W6
Philistines, people. 11, 12:W6
Philoteria, *Beth-yerah.* 23, 26, 27:X4
Phoenicia, region. 4, 14, 15, 23, 25, 26, 27, 28:X2; 8:B3; 13:H4; 16:G4; 31:H6
Phoenix, *Porto Loutro.* 33:B5
Phrygia, region. 16:F2; 32, 33:C1; 37:G3
Phibeseth, (Bubastis), *T. Basta.* 10:A5
Pisidia, region. 32, 33:C2
Pithom, *T. er-Retabeh.* 10:B4
Po, (Padus), river. 22:B1
Polemon, Kingdom of. 32, 33:D1
Pontus, region. 21, 22:D1; 37:H3
Port Said. 39:B4
Port Tawfiq. 39:B5
Prophthasia, *Qala-i-Kang.* 20:F3
Propontis. 32, 33:B1
Psephinus Tower, in Jerusalem. 34
Pteria, *Bogazkoy.* 18:C2
Ptolemaic Kingdom. 21, 22:C2
Ptolemais, (Acco, Acre), *T. el-Fukhkhar.* 23, 25, 26, 27, 28, 35, 38:X3; 31:G7; 32, 33:D3
Punon, *Feinan.* 10:E5; 13:H7
Pura, *Fahraj.* 18, 20:F4
Puteoli, (Pozzuoli). 33:A4; 36:D3

Q

Qarqar, *Kh. Qarqur.* 16:G3
Qatna, *T. el-Mishrifiyeh.* 9:G3
Qiryat Gat. 39:D3
Qiryat Yam. 39:D2
Qumran, (City of Salt), *Kh. Qumran.* 12, 23, 25, 26, 28, 35, 38:X6; *see also city plan p. 34*

R

Raamses, *see* Ramses
Rabbah, (Philadelphia), *Amman.* 4, 11, 12, 14, 19, 23, 38:Y5; 8:C5; 10:E3; 13:H6
Rafah, (Raphia). 39:D4
Ragaba, Rajib. 23:Y3

Ramah, *er-Ram.* 12, 15, 19:X6
Rām Allāh. 39:D3
Ramat Gam. 39:D3
Ramathaim, (Arimathea), *Rentis.* 23:X5
Ramat Rahel. 38:X6
Ramla. 39:D3
Ramoth-gilead, *T. Ramith.* 11, 12, 14, 15:Z4; 13:H5
Ramses, *Qantir.* 10:A4
Raphana, *er-Rafeh.* 25, 26:Z3
Raphia, *Rafah.* 4, 15, 19, 23, 26, 35:V7; 13:G6; 16:F4
Raphon, *er-Rafeh.* 23:Z3
Ra's an Naqb. 39:E5
Ra's as Sidr. 39:B5
Ras Feshkha. 34:X6
Ra's Ghārib. 39:C7
Ra's Shukheir. 39:C7
Red Sea. 9, 16:G6; 10, 39:C7; 17, 18, 20:C4; 21, 22:B2
Rehob, *T. el-Gharbi.* 11:X3
Rephidim, *Wadi Refayid* (?). 10:C7
Reuben, tribe. 11:Y6
Rhagae, *Reyy.* 18, 20:E2
Rhegium, *Reggio.* 33:A5
Rhine, river. 37:D1
Rhodes, island. 8, 16:E3; 18, 32, 33:B2; 21, 22:C1
Rhossus. 37:H4
Riblah, *Ribleh.* 17:C3
Rome. 21, 22:B1; 33:A4; 36:D3; *see also city plan p. 24, illust. p. 24, 36*
Royal Portico, in Jerusalem. 25, 29
Rumah, *Kh. Rumeh.* 15:X4

S

St. Catherine's Monastery. 39:C7
Sais, *San el-Hagar.* 16:F4; 17, 18:B3
Saka, (Scythians), people. 19, 21:G1
Salamis, north of *Famagusta.* 31:F4; 33:D2; 37:H4
Salecah, *Salkhad.* 13:J5
Salim, *Umm el-'Amdan.* 26, 28:X5
Salmone, Cape, *Cape Sidheros.* 33:C5
Salona, Salonae, 24:D2; 36:E2
Salt, City of, *Qumran.* 12:W6
Salt Sea, (Dead Sea). 4, 11, 12, 14, 15, 19, 23:X6; 8:B6; 13:H6
Samaga, *es-Samik.* 23:Y6
Samal, *Zinjirli.* 16:G3
Samaria, region. 4, 19, 23, 25, 26, 28, 35:X5; 31:G7
Samaria, (Sebaste), *Sebastiyeh.* 4, 15, 19, 23, 25, 38:X5; 16:G4; *see illust. p. 21*
Samosata, *Samsat.* 37:H3
Samothrace, island. 32,33:B2
Sanāfīr. 39:D7
Sangarius, river. 8:F1
Saragossa, (Caesarea Augusta). 36:B2
Sardinia. 21, 22:B1
Sardis, *Sart.* 16:E2; 17, 18, 20:B2; 32, 33:B1; 37:G3
Sarepta, (Zarephath), *Sarafand.* 26, 28:X2
Saudi Arabia, nation. 39:E7
Scythians, people. 17, 18:B1
Scythians, (Saka), people. 17:E1; 18, 21:G1
Scythopolis, (Beth-shan), *T. el-Husn.* 23, 25, 26, 27, 28, 35, 38:X4; 31:G7
Sebaste, (Samaria), *Sebastiyeh.* 25, 26, 28, 35, 38:X5; 31:G8
Second Quarter, in Jerusalem. 25, 29, 34
Sede Boqer. 39:D4
Sedom. 39:E4

Seir, *see* Edom.
Sela, *Umm el-Bayyarah* (?), possibly *es-Sela'.* 10:E5; 13:H7; 16:G5
Seleucia, in Mesopotamia near *Baghdad.* 21, 22:E1
Seleucia, *Seliqiyeh,* in Gaulanitis. 23, 27, 35:Y3
Seleucia, *Silifke,* in Cilicia. 31:F1; 37:H4
Seleucia Pieria, *Seluqiyeh.* 32, 33:D2; 31:H3
Seleucid Kingdom. 21, 22:D1; 23:Z2
Semechonitis, Lake, (L. Hula). 27:Y3
Sennabris, *Sinn en-Nabra.* 35:X4
Seph, *Safed.* 35:X3
Sepphoris, *Saffuriyeh.* 23, 25, 26, 27, 28, 35, 38:X4
Serabit el-Khadim. 10:C6
Serbal, Jebel, mt. 10:C7
Serpent's Pool, in Jerusalem. 29
Sevan, Lake. 16:J2
Shaalbim, Selbit. 11, 14:X6
Sharm ash Shaykh. 39:D7
Sharon, Plain of. 4, 11, 12, 14, 15, 19, 23, 25, 26:W5
Sharuhen, *T. el-Fa'ra.* 8:A7
Schechem, (Sichem), *T. Balata.* 4, 11, 12, 14, 15, 19, 38:X5; 8:B5; 10:D3; 13:G6; *see illust. p. 11*
Shephelah, "the Lowland". 4, 12:W6
Shibīn al Kawm. 39:A5
Shikmona. 38:W4
Shiloh, *Seilun.* 4, 11, 12, 15, 19:X5; 8:B5; 10:D3
Shimron, *T. Semuniyeh.* 11, 12, 14:X4
Shittim, (Abel-shittim), *T. el-Matba'.* 15:Y6
Shunem, *Solem.* 15:X4
Shur, Wilderness of. 10:C4
Sichem, (Shechem), *T. Balata.* 23:X5
Sicily. 21, 22:B1; 33:A5; 36:D3
Sidon region. 19:X2
Sidon, *Saida.* 4, 11, 12, 14, 15, 19, 23, 25, 26, 28, 38:X2; 8:B3; 13:H4; 16:G4; 31:G6; 32, 33:D3; 37:H4; 39:D1
Sidonians, people. 11, 12:X2
Siloam, Pool of, in Jerusalem. 18, 22, 25, 29
Simeon, tribe. 11:W7
Sin, (Pelusium), *T. Farama.* 10:B4
Sin, Wilderness of. 10:C6
Sinai, region. 9:F5
Sinai, Mt., *J. Musa.* 10, 39:C7
Sinai Peninsula. 10:C6; 13:F8; 39:C5
Sinope. 16:G1; 17, 18, 20:C1; 37:H3
Sippar, *Abu Habbah.* 9:J4; 16:J4; 17, 18:D3
Sirbon, Lake. 10:C4
Sitifi. 36:C4
Siut. *Asyut.* 16:F5
Siwa, (Temple of Amon), oasis. 18:A3
Smyrna, *Izmir.* 32, 33:B1; 37:F3
Soco, Socoh, *T. er-Ras,* in Solomon's 3rd district. 14, 15:X5
Socoh, *Kh. 'Abbad,* in Judah. 12:W6
Sodom, southern end of Dead Sea (?). 8:B7
Sogane, *Sakhnin.* 35:X3
Sogane, *Yahudiya.* 35:Y3
Sogdiana, region. 18, 21:F2
Solomon's Porch, in Jerusalem. 25, 29
Sorek, *Wadi es-Sarar,* valley. 4, 12:W6; 8:A6
Sapin, region. 36:B2

Sparta. 17, 18, 20, 32, 33:A2; 36:F4
Strato's Tower, (Caesarea). 19, 23, 25:W4
Subeita. 38:W8
Succoth, *T. Deir 'alla.* 8:B5; 11, 12, 14, 15, 38:Y5; 13:H6
Succoth, *T. el-Maskhuta,* in Egypt. 10, 39:B5
Suez. 39:B5
Suez Canal. 39:B4
Suez, Gulf of. 10, 39:C7
Sumer, region. 9:J4
Sumur. 8:C1
Susa, (Shushan), *Shush.* 9, 16:K4; 17, 18, 20:D3
Susiana, region. 18, 20:D3
Sychar, *T. Balatah.* 26, 28:X5
Syene, (Elephantine), *Aswan.* 16:F6; 17, 18, 20:B4
Syracuse. 21, 22:B1; 33:A5; 36:E4
Syria, nation. 39:E2
Syria, region. 16:G4; 17, 20:C3; 21, 22:B1; 26:Y2; 31:J4; 35:X2; 37:H4
Syrian Desert. 13:K4

T

Taanach, *T. Ta'annek.* 8:B5; 10:D3; 11, 12, 14, 15, 38:X4; 13:G5
Tāba. 39:D6
Taberah. 10:C6
Tabgha, *et-Tabghah.* 27, 38:X3
Tabor, Mt., *Jebel et-Tur.* 4, 11, 12, 14, 15, 23, 26, 27, 28, 35:X4; *see illust. p. 11*
Tadmor, (Palmyra), *Tudmur.* 9:H3; 13:K3; 16:H4
Tamar, *Ain el-'Arus* (?). 11, 12, 14, 15:X8; 13:G7
Tanis, (Zoan), *San el-Hagar.* 10, 39:A4; 16:F4
Tannur. 39:E4
Tantā. 39:A4
Tarabulus, (Tripoli). 39:E1
Tarfā, Wadi at. 39:A7
Taricheae, (Magadan), *Mejdel.* 25, 35:X4
Tarsus, *Tarsus.* 16:G3; 17, 18, 20:B2; 31:G2; 32, 33:D1; 33:D5; 37:H4
Tatta, Lake. 32, 33:D1
Taurus Mts. 9, 16:F3
Taxila, *Takshacila.* 19, 21:G3
Tekoa, *Kh. Tequ.'* 12, 15, 19, 23:X6
Tel Aviv-Yafo. 39:D3
Teleilat el-Ghassul. 38:Y6
Tell Abu Hawam. 38:X4
Tell Abu Matar. 38:W7
Tell 'Aitun, (Eglon?). 38:W7
Tell Anafa. 38:Y3
Tell 'Arad, (Arad). 34, 38:X7
Tell Beit Mirsim. 38:X7
Tell Brak. 9:H3
Tell Deir 'alla, (Succoth). 8:B5; 38:Y5
Tell el-'Ajjul. 38:W7
Tell el-Amarna. 8:E5
Tell el-'Areini. 38:W6
Tell el-Far'ah, (Sharuhen) 38:W7
Tell el-Far'ah, (Tirzah). 38:X5
Tell el-Hayyat. 38:Y5
Tell el-Hesi, (Eglon?). 8:A6; 38:W6; *see illust. p. 38*
Tell el-Jurn, (En-gedi). 34:X7
Tell el-Qasileh. 38:W5
Tell en-Nasbeh, (Mizpah?). 38:X6
Tell en-Nejileh. 38:W7
Tell esh-Sheri'ah. 38:W7
Tell es-Safi, (Libnah). 38:W8
Tell es-Saidiyeh, (Zarethan?). 38:Y5
Tell es-Seba (Beer-sheba). 38:W7
Tell es-Sultan, O. T. Jericho. 34:X6

Picture Credits

The editor and publisher wish to express their thanks and appreciation to the following for supplying illustrations:

The American Numismatic Society, New York: pages 20 (bottom), 21 (top right), 22 (center left), 28 (bottom right), 29 (bottom left), 35 (bottom right). Henry Angelo-Castrillon: page 32 (top right), 36 (right). The Bettmann Archive, New York: page 42. The Trustees of the British Museum: pages 16 (all three photos), 18 (top). Ernest J. Dupuy: pages 32 (top left), 36 (center), 37 (center). GAF Pana-Vue Slides: pages 24 (top), 28 (top). Hebrew University, Jerusalem, Department of Archaeology: page 22 (bottom right). Iran National Tourist Office, New York: page 18 (left). Israel Government Tourist Office, New York: title page, pages 5 (bottom left), 11 (top), 27 (left), 29 (top left), 30 (second from top), 35 (two photos at top). The Israel Museum, Jerusalem: pages 11 (top right), 14 (top right), 18 (bottom right), 28 (bottom left). Istanbul Museum: page 30 (top). Italian Government Travel Office: page 36 (left). Nancy L. Lapp: page 12. From Lepsius, *Denkmaeler*: page 10 (right). Herbert G. May: page 27 (bottom right). The Metropolitan Museum of Art: pages 2, 22 (top left and top right), 37 (bottom right). Museo Nazionale, Naples: pages 20 (top), 21 (center right). Museum of Fine Arts, Boston: page 24 (bottom). Notre Dame de Sion, Jerusalem: page 29 (center bottom). The Oriental Institute, University of Chicago: pages 17, 38 (center). The University Museum, University of Pennsylvania: pages 9, 37 (left). Wide World Photos: page 30 (third from top).

Photographs from collection of Professor Harry Thomas Frank: pages 5 (three photos at right), 7 (both), 8, 10 (left), 11 (bottom), 14 (top left), 21 (top left), 22 (center right and bottom left), 25, 27 (center and top right), 29 (center top and right), 30 (bottom), 35 (bottom left), 38 (top two photos and bottom photo).